Surfing

WOMEN OF THE WAVES

Surfing
WOMEN OF THE WAVES

LINDA CHASE   PHOTOGRAPHS BY ELIZABETH PEPIN

Gibbs Smith, Publisher
TO ENRICH AND INSPIRE HUMANKIND
Salt Lake City | Charleston | Santa Fe | Santa Barbara

First Edition

12 11 10 09 08   5 4 3 2 1

Text © 2008 Linda Chase

Photographs © 2008 Elizabeth Pepin

Published by
Gibbs Smith, Publisher
P.O. Box 667
Layton, Utah 84041

Orders: 1.800.835.4993
www.gibbs-smith.com

Designed by Ryan Christopher
Printed and bound in China

Library of Congress Cataloging-in-Publication Data

Chase, Linda.
  Surfing : women of the waves / Linda Chase ; photographs by Elizabeth
Pepin. — 1st ed.
      p. cm.
  ISBN-13: 978-1-4236-0179-1
  ISBN-10: 1-4236-0179-3
  1. Women surfers. I. Title.

GV839.7.W65C43 2007
797.3'2092—dc22

                              2007033841

CONTENTS

I could not possibly acknowledge all the people who helped to prepare me for writing this book and provided their support and encouragement, but there are a few whose invaluable contributions deserve special thanks:

Gibbs Smith, the publisher, for providing me with the opportunity to write this book; Elizabeth Pepin, principal photographer and invaluable collaborator; my editor, Katie Newbold, and the talented crew at Gibbs Smith; Mary Pat Koos, who instructed me, where needed, to "fix this sentence!"; Sid Stebel, my writing mentor, and the members of the Wednesday night writer's group, a faithful and supportive lot if ever there was one; and, of course, all of the women surfers whose generosity and humor and passion and extraordinary talent form the heart and soul of this book.

Why Do Women Surf?

IN THE CHILLY PRE-DAWN, WOMEN THE WORLD OVER STRUGGLE AWAKE AND MAKE WHISPERED CALLS, AN URGENT SINGLE-MINDED QUESTION: IS IT GOOD TODAY?

AND THE WHISPERED ANSWER COMES, JOYOUSLY, EAGERLY: TODAY IT IS GOOD.

And so we cast aside the sacred rituals of womanhood. We put down our long to-do lists —give birth, drive kids to soccer, fix dinner, climb corporate ladder, clean glass ceiling. Young girls abandon their Barbies. Executives part painfully with their cell phones and Blackberries. Grandmothers stow their knitting. Lifelong night people become early morning people.

From Cornwall to Cardiff-by-the-Sea, Malibu to Waimea Bay, we heed the clarion call:

Surf's up.

Why do women surf? For the same reasons as men:

To experience danger and exhilaration.

To get an adrenaline high.

To commune with nature.

To satisfy a primal longing to reunite with the sea.

To experience, however momentarily, freedom, pleasure, and liberation from our mundane lives.

To find God.

What joy, what unfettered bliss, to ride upon a wave, to follow its rushing curvature to the shore.

Women also surf for different reasons than men:

Because our boyfriends surf.

Because we are young and fearless and want to live on the edge.

Because we are middle-aged and afraid that the recliner is coming to claim us.

Because we discover that shopping and yoga and chocolate, while still necessary, are no longer sufficient.

Because we are girls and want to be women.

Because we are women and want to be girls.

Because we yearn to lose ourselves in the waves. Or to find ourselves.

Because someone said we can.

Because someone said we can't.

From the California coast to the North Shore of Oahu, from Australia to South Africa—anywhere there are waves—you will find women surfing.

CHAPTER 1

GIRL *on the Shore*

SURFING, FOR MANY YEARS, WAS AN UNAPOLOGETICALLY MASCULINE CULTURE, A KIND OF AQUATIC LOCKER ROOM TO WHICH WOMEN WERE NOT ADMITTED. As the official counter-culture sport of the '60s, surfing was not just a sport but a lifestyle, one long, sun-drenched beach party with endless waves and music. Surfing was widely considered the epitome of cool, and all the more delicious because it engendered the disapproval of teachers, parents and other authority figures. Girls were largely decorative objects, relegated to cheering on the boys from the shore and making beer runs.

The songs of the surf culture—the Ventures, the Surfaris, the Deltones, the Beach Boys—contained the encoding of the surfing culture: dress, hairstyles, lingo, even gender roles. The Beach Boys' wistful 1963 ballad, "Surfer Girl," made it manifestly clear that a girl's place was on the shore. We are spotted there, standing by the ocean roar, yet, we are assured, if we play our cards right, we might surf together, and, in his woody he will take us everywhere he goes. Other songs provided additional clues: in the calculus of the surfing culture, for example, there would be two girls for every boy.

The reality of the '60s surf culture could be as chilly as the cold Pacific currents lurking beneath the water's surface. In the bleak damp of California's June gloom, lanky boys went down to the water with their boards, and the girls sat on the beach on their towels, shivering in hopes that the sun would eventually appear so that their tans would be smooth and even. The girls could wax the boards and go for hamburgers and beer, but riding the waves was for the boys.

Kia'i Tallett is stoked as she paddles out with her mother on the Big Island of Hawai'i.

Those of us who carry the X chromosome are not inexperienced in reading between the lines, decoding cultural signals about our roles. From the time we are in the womb, we absorb our instructions, identifying our place in the world: Never wear horizontal stripes. Throw like a girl. And a whole series of proscriptives: Can't. Don't. Shouldn't. Musn't.

Not that girls aren't genetically endowed for certain tasks, some of which are no mean feats. As little girls, we fired up our Easy-Bake Ovens, creating little miracle cakes from the faint heat of a single lightbulb. As women, we can, if prompted, create our own seas of amniotic fluid, and nine months later, produce a human being.

But when it comes to throwing a ball or racing down a track or riding a wave, those are things best left to the boys. Sunbathing is acceptable, even desirable ("and the girls all get so tan"), and swimming in the ocean is permitted. But the ocean is capricious and wild; out there battling the waves is no place, surely, for a girl.

This notion has been disproved by generations of female surfers, from **Linda Benson** and **Joyce Hoffman** in the '50s and '60s to **Layne Beachley**, **Sofia Mulanovich**, and others in the new millennium. However, the women struggle even today to earn respect in the surf lineup. Even the great **Lisa Andersen**, four-time women's world champion in the '90s, is sometimes greeted with

Riding the waves in Waikiki, with the Royal Hawaiian in the background.

hostility—until she takes off on a wave, that is. She knows the rules—and she also knows that you have to prove yourself not once but many times, and that respect comes grudgingly and is hard-earned.

Women have always had an inexorable connection with the sea. The female figure and its powerful connection to the life-giving force of the sea occur frequently in art and mythology. In Botticelli's rendering of the birth of Venus (circa 1480), the Roman goddess of love is depicted rising full-blown from the sea, standing in glorious full nudity on a pink half shell, hair flowing about her. She was blown to shore by the Zephyrs, and is about to be draped with a mantle by one of the Hours. The rounded form, the classical pose, conveys a sensuality—a sense of light and balletic movement—prefiguring the images hundred of years later of female Hawaiians poised upon their boards, surfing in the nude.

Mermaids, who possess the torso of a woman and tail of a fish, occur frequently in myth and fable. By virtue of their aquatic appendage, they can move about freely in the ocean, unencumbered by earthbound obligations—which is surely part of the appeal of surfing. Not that any of us wants to grow prehensile fins, but we envy the mermaid's close affinity with the sea.

Mythical or real flesh-and-blood women have, over the years, acquitted themselves well in the water. They swim, they water-ski—sometimes singly, sometimes stacked in pyramids—they compete in athalons, they catapult themselves off high dives and they perform intricate water routines. Some, an intrepid few, go beyond the accepted boundaries, performing great feats of athleticism and endurance in the water.

On an August morning in 1926, **Gertrude Ederle** set out to become the first woman to swim the English Channel. Hour after grueling hour, the eighteen-year-old battled cold, fatigue, nausea and heavy seas in the arduous twenty-one-mile swim from Cape Gris Nez to Dover. After twelve hours, someone on the boat that was accompanying her leaned over the side and shouted to her, "Trudy, you must come out!" And Trudy raised her head out of the water and shouted back, "What for?" She completed the swim in fourteen hours and thirty-one minutes, surpassing the time of the fastest man by two hours.

Esther Williams, the champion-swimmer-turned-movie-star, made elaborately choreographed swimming numbers look effortless. In actuality, she was putting herself at risk each time she performed. While filming the lavish finale for the 1952 film *Million-Dollar Mermaid*, Williams dove off a fifty-foot platform and broke her neck. She spent the next six months in a body cast. In the course of her movie career, she also suffered several punctured eardrums and near drownings, yet there was this thing inside that drove her, whether the quest for immortality or the need to master over and over this physical challenge.

The mermaid mystique survives at Florida's Weeki Wachee Springs, where Sativa Smith performs as a mermaid, swimming for forty-five minutes straight while lip-synching to music and holding her breath for up to two and a half minutes at a stretch. Even without the lip-synching, this surely qualifies her for the Mermaid Hall of Fame.

From left to right: Surfing Waikiki, with Diamond Head in the background; Holly Beck free surfing, Roxy Jam, Cardiff, California; Mary Osborne lights up a wave in Ventura, California; Girls NSAA Contest, Kona, Hawai'i.

These water women have demonstrated to a world of skeptics and doubters that women have the physical stamina and mental toughness to perform all sorts of feats in both pool and ocean. They achieved a kind of immortality, but not without a cost.

Following her triumphant swim, Ederle was engulfed by an outpouring of public adulation, yet because of greed and shortsightedness by her handlers, it never translated into financial gain. She hurt her back in an aquatic demonstration and spent eight months in a cast; later, consigned to the footlights of history, she found herself giving swimming lessons. As for Williams, she lives forever in celluloid, but her screen exploits diminish in this age of computer enhancement; she seems less a flesh-and-blood person than a mythical creature, a mermaid, perhaps, who lives in the water and emerges from time to time to entertain us.

Ederle's and Williams's names can readily be summoned from the dim recesses of schoolbook memories—however, the names of surfers cannot be so readily recalled. One would think that, with the oceans covering 70 percent of the earth's surface, there would be ample room for women on the surf line. However, the best surf breaks are only found in a few

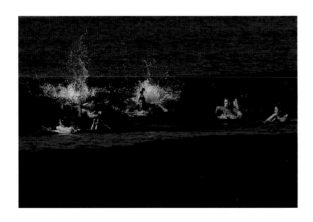

select places, and those, for the most part, had already been commandeered by the boys. It was as though the ocean was a tree house or fort, occupied by boys, carrying a crudely lettered sign: KEEP OUT.

Fortunately, there were a few young women who were not content to stand on the shore and watch the boys shoot the curl and hang ten. They took up their boards and paddled out and claimed their rightful place in the surf, proving to the world that women of flesh and bone, not just the creatures of myth, belonged to the sea and the sea to them. They broke down the door to the clubhouse with grace and agility and guts, proving that girls could do this, too, and do it very well.

Women surfers were not readily received into what had been a largely exclusive all-boys club. Those who had the sheer audacity to paddle out and take their place in the lineup were often greeted with derision and insults: "Come back when your tits are bigger," Jericho Poppler was

One summer's day: Judith Cohen (top) and Summer Romero (bottom) strut their stuff.

told. Others were met with threats, even physical violence. In the '70s, pro surfer Sally Prange was punched in the face by an irate male surfer at Ala Moana, on Oahu's South Shore. In another incident, a California woman surfing with her friends at Ala Moana inadvertently took off in front of a male surfer. He tried to force her off the wave, but she managed to work her way into a fast hollow section of wave and rode in, leaving him fuming in the white water. He was waiting for her when she paddled back out. He ordered her and her friends to leave and never return. "If I catch you out here again," he said, "I'll shove my board right up your cunt."

The use of the "C word"—a shocking, almost physical assault—is a measure of the hostility that female surfers have encountered. As women surfers increase in numbers and their proficiency grows, they have begun to earn the grudging respect of the guys. Even in the enlightened new millennium, the highest compliment that could be paid to a female surfer is, "She surfs as good as a guy." When six-time world champion Lisa Andersen drops into a wave at Huntington, or Tiare Thomas goes tandem surfing with her partner Bobby Friedman on a fifteen-foot face at

Kalani Talentino divides her surfing between Hawai'i and California.

Backdoor Pipe, experienced male surfers are heard to remark, "Whoa!" or "Holy shit, you went out in that?"

Today, women of all ages and skill levels have taken their place among the waves. Longboarders, shortboarders, goofyfooters, hotdoggers, shredders, big-wave mavens, soul surfers, young girls who dance upon their boards like ballerinas, surfer moms, middle-aged novices who can barely get out of bed in the morning, triumphantly stand up on a surfboard for the first time—in the water! These are the women of the waves, and their numbers are growing every day. Indeed, after golf, surfing is the fastest-growing women's sport. Not just in California and Hawai'i, but in Mexico and Peru, Australia and South Africa, even Ireland and chilly Cornwall, women are attending surf clinics and camps, bravely donning wet suits with names like Body Glove that protect them from the cold, paddling out and joining the surf lineup, waiting their turn patiently, as is their wont. Others are following in the long, illustrious line of professional surfers, competing all over the world, pushing themselves and each other to new limits.

Kristen Steiner makes it look easy.

Surfing beats the mall any day.

Today, the notion of a girl standing on the shore, working on her tan and watching her boyfriend surf, seems as antiquated as woolen bathing costumes and wooden surfboards. Susan Orlean, whose best-selling book *Orchid Thief* inspired the movie *Adaptation*, wrote an article, "Surf Girls of Maui," that inspired another film—*Blue Crush*, the definitive girls' surfer movie. In observing the surfer girls in Hana, a little town at the end of a long road on Maui, Orleans noted, "To be a surfer girl is even cooler, wilder, and more modern than being a guy surfer. . . . To be a surfer girl is to be all that surfing represents, plus the extra charge of being a girl in a tough guy's domain."

As the surfer on the right discovers, women like Mary Bagalso are claiming their share of the waves.

The coolness, the wildness, the unmistakable aura of sexuality, these are part of surfing's ineffable appeal. Even those of us who have amassed a few more years find ourselves drawn to surfing, perhaps to express our wildness, to find that elemental connection to nature that has been lost in the jangle and clamor of modern life. In ever-growing numbers, we join the legions of the women of the waves.

FOR TO SURF IS TO BE EXALTED AMONG MORTALS; TO SURF WELL IS TO TAKE ONE'S PLACE AMONG THE GODS.*

Wipeout: A Surfing Lesson on the North Shore

It was the morning of the first day of the rest of my life, or the last. I was on the North Shore of Oahu, in winter, heading out for my first surfing lesson. Already I could hear the mocking laughter of the Surfaris:

Ha-ha-ha-ha-ha-Wipeout!

Until that moment, I had put surfing in the category of other supposedly fun things I would never do: dance the pas des deux from *Swan Lake*; play center court at Wimbledon; be catapulted into space. It was all well and good for Gidget—she looked like Sandra Dee and used the word "bitchen" in the most alluring way. **But I was fifty-five, not fifteen, and not blessed with one whit of athletic ability; in fact, I trip walking on berber carpet.**

Yet here I was, staring down the one- to two-foot sets at Haleiwa, wondering what folly was this. The previous year, I had made a pilgrimage to the North Shore to see the big waves. The crazy surfers were there in droves, lining up for the annual Quiksilver Big Wave Invitational in Memory of Eddie Aikau, for which the waves have to be at least twenty feet. The day I went, they were a mere fifteen, and so the surfers paced on the shore and the vendors peddled T-shirts. I bought one that read "Banzai Pipeline: Man and Nature in Harmony." Those waves did not look as though they were interested in harmonizing with anyone; dissonance seemed more their note. The next day, when the waves hit twenty feet and the Eddie Aikau got underway, I was on a plane back to California.

Three surfers head down to catch a wave at Turtle Bay on Oahu's North Shore.

Something must have happened to me that day, some surfing virus must have been slipped into my Hawaiian shave ice because the following year I was back, and this time I was actually going to attempt to reverse the immutable laws of nature and stand up on a surfboard in moving water.

The morning of my lesson, it was raining and the ocean was a surly gray. I wandered over to the Hans Hedemann Surf School at Turtle Bay Resort, hoping to learn that the lesson had been canceled, but no. The tall girl behind the counter gave me a baleful look and handed me a nylon pullover in a particularly unbecoming shade of mustard. Called a rash shirt, this garment had a strictly utilitarian function: to protect against sunburn, coral scrapings, etc.; however, as a fashion statement, it left much to be desired.

We piled into a van and headed out for Haleiwa, about fifteen minutes west. The driver was one of Hans's instructors, a young blond kid, and my fellow passengers included two Australian teenagers with their dad. The boys were having their first lesson also, but, the dad assured me, they were expert boogie boarders and bodysurfers and should have no problem. Great, I thought darkly, the bloody Aussies will pop up on their boards the first time and I'll fall off mine with the grace and panache of a sack of cement; surfing dogs will pass by, grinning.

As the van came around the hairpin turn at Waimea Bay, I looked out at the waves. They weren't Eddie Aikau twenty-footers, but they looked plenty big. "Where are we headed?" I asked nervously. The driver grinned. "Pipeline."

Oh Lord, why did I not stay in bed with my P. D. James mystery and read about more agreeable ways of meeting your demise, like a cup of arsenic or a poison dart? Even though we did not stop at Pipeline, I felt my nerves jumping at the looming physical challenge before me. I had had certain successes in my time—I still bask in the glory of my fifth-grade spelling championship—but none of these endeavors had prepared me for what lay ahead.

At Haleiwa, the bay forms a protective shield from the big waves forming out in the open water. As our little group assembled on the beach, the clouds parted and a warm Hawaiian sun broke through. **We were given a few safety rules, and then we practiced lying down on the board, pushing up with our arms and then getting up, all in one fluid motion. It's hard enough popping up on land when the board isn't moving; what happens when you're out there on the water and trying to clamber up on this floating, heaving peace of foam? Keep your weight low and balanced, we were instructed.** I was thinking more of how to gracefully execute a wipeout: something graceful and Esther Williams-ish.

"I just don't want to be the worst surfing student ever," I told Hans, who was to be my personal instructor. Presented with this lofty goal, he assured me that to qualify for that, I would have to not go out.

I stood face to face with a rather large body of water, the Pacific Ocean, with nothing to break the rolling swells building in from the north. These were only one- to two-foot waves, but they seemed much larger, rising up, readying themselves for me. But there was Hans, with his misplaced faith in me, and the Aussie kids; I had to hold up the side. This will be my lasting legacy to the North Shore: **Not the Worst Surfing Student Ever.**

We marched with our boards to the water's edge and paddled out . . . and out . . . and out. The waves were coming in fast sets, promising a spirited test of whatever surfing bones I might have in my body.

This surf student is tearing it up!

The junior instructor was assigned to the Aussies, and Hans took me in tow, guiding me to a part of the bay where the breaks were coming in long, smooth swells. "From zero to hero," he promised me. "You need the attitude of wanting to go for it."

He turned me around on my board so that I was facing the shore. The next thing I heard was his shout: "Stand up!"

I crouched, clinging to the board for dear life, as it skimmed in toward the shore. Then, slowly, I let go and started to rise up.

WIPEOUT!

One minute I was this surfing diva, and the next, I was thrown from the board and tumbled into the ocean. Fortunately, the water cushioned my fall, and buoyed by subcutaneous body fat, I popped up, still conscious, no bones broken, spinal cord still as one.

Hans and I floated and watched the Aussies have a go. The boys nimbly leapt up on their boards, but they, too, suffered spectacular wipeouts.

"They stood up too straight," Hans informed me, "a common mistake of beginners."

Before my next attempt, he imparted his teaching philosophy: "Keep it simple." He offered a trifecta of things to think about: keep your eyes on the shore, keep your weight low and balanced, and don't let go of the board until your feet are in position. Three things . . . I can remember three things.

Eyes on the shore, eyes on the shore.

"Stand up!"

Keep your weight low.

No problem there—as long as I remained on all fours and didn't attempt to emulate homo erectus, I was just fine. Don't look down. (I was navigating these new ideas as the board, on its own volition, went rocketing toward the shore.) Now . . . now . . . let go . . . get up.

It was a miracle of nature, a defiance of all natural law. I was standing on a surfboard, riding the waves, not in the curl exactly, but moving in an exhilaration rush of speed toward the shore.

Then I looked down, and the ride came to an abrupt halt.

I surfaced in a spray of white sea foam just as Hans came skimming by on his board, looking as relaxed and at ease as if he were riding on a moving sidewalk. He could've been drinking a cup of coffee and reading the paper.

He finished his ride and paddled back out to me. "You looked down," he said.

"I know." A rookie mistake—won't happen again. Of course, it did.

More attempts, more wipeouts. **I repeated Hans's three-step mantra, and finally, through some harmonic convergence of wave, board and body, it happened: At Hans's command, I pushed up, got my feet in position and rose up, wobbling wildly, arms flailing for balance, feet inching for optimal position, eyes on the shore—then suddenly, my board and I were as one, riding the wild surf.** I made it into shore and hopped off, as though I'd been doing this every day my entire life.

**Eyes on the shore,
and enjoy the ride!**

Hans seemed not particularly surprised by my surfing triumph. He had faith, if not in this problematic student, then in his "keep-it-simple" approach. We spent a couple of hours at it, catching the waves (Hans did all the selecting; I merely went on his command). I had a few more good rides and many more spectacular wipeouts, worthy of the agony-of-defeat moment on *Wide World of Sports.*

Finally, exhausted, scanning the shore for the Ibuprofen stand, I decided to call it a day.

Patiently waiting for the next wave.

"One more," Hans said.

All right, one more. For Hans.

You want the last ride of the day to be the best. It wasn't—but still, I was pleased with my first-ever surfing adventure. Back on the beach, a girl in her twenties spotted me. "You were tearing it up out there," she said.

"Well, no," I demurred, but inwardly I was beaming—I was tearing it up! ✳

A surf sister celebrates!

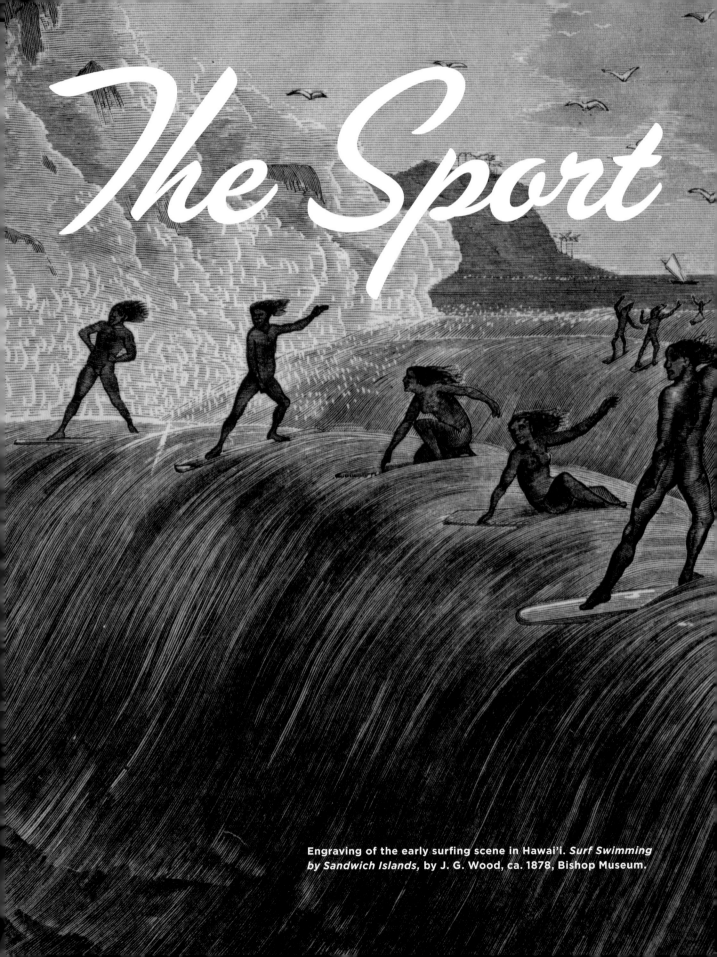

The Sport

Engraving of the early surfing scene in Hawai'i. *Surf Swimming by Sandwich Islands,* by J. G. Wood, ca. 1878, Bishop Museum.

# of Queens

THAT SURFING EVOLVED INTO SUCH A DISTINCTLY MACHO CULTURE IS DOUBLY IRONIC GIVEN THAT IN HAWAI'I, WHERE SURFING'S ANCIENT ROOTS RESIDE, MEN AND WOMEN ENJOYED EQUALITY IN THE WAVES. Nathaniel Emerson, writing in 1892, found that surfing possessed "the vitality of a national pastime" and that "the zest of the sport was enhanced by the fact that both sexes engaged in it." The sport of kings (and queens) was the special prerogative of the *ali'i* (royalty), who delighted in demonstrating their daring and skill on the waves. **Women competed in surf contests along with men, frequently carrying off the highest honors.** Courtships were conducted in the surf, great romances often rising (and falling) on the suitor's skill at handling himself on the waves without breaking any *kapu* (taboos).

Hawaiian mythology, passed down through oral tradition, abounds with tales of love and vengeance involving surfers—men and women. Kelea, the beautiful sister of Maui's ruling chief and considered among the most graceful, daring surfers in the kingdom, was abducted in an outrigger canoe and forced to become the wife of Lolale, high chief of Oahu. Lolale was not one for surfing or anything else related to the sea, and landlocked Kelea yearned for her beloved ocean, slipping away to surf at the white beaches at 'Ewa. Finally, her husband, recognizing her unhappiness, gave his consent for her return to Maui. She stopped at 'Ewa and joined the other nobles sporting themselves in the surf, and such was her skill that she bested all the chiefs. The onlookers' cheers drew the attention of Kalamakua, the high chief of the region. He threw his mantle over her shoulders when she emerged from the surf, and she became his wife.

Mamala, a *kapua* (demigoddess) who could take the form of a lizard, shark or woman, was also renowned for her surfing prowess. **She was known to surf in rough waves of Ke-kai-o-Mamala, the surf break west of what is now Waikiki. She was married to Ouha, another kapua, but left him for Honoka'upu, the coconut grove chief. Spurned by his surfing goddess, Ouha cast off his human form and became a shark god, prowling the waters between Waikiki and Koko Head.**

The ali'i had the run of the waves, and woe be to the surfer who dared to ride the same waves as a high-ranking chief or chiefess. One day, in the surf off Waikiki, Pikoi, a surfer of considerable skill, found himself surfing the same wave as the wife of the island's ruling chief. Realizing he had broken the kapu against surfing the same wave as a member of royalty, he tried to cut across to another wave, but she caught that one as well, and they rode to shore together. The crowd on the beach grabbed him and was ready to kill him. It was owing to his proficiency as a rat-killer (he skewered four hundred of the rodents with one shot of his arrow)—and the fact that he was the brother-in-law of one of the chiefs—that his life was spared.

European contact produced the first written account of surf-riding in the Islands. **In 1777, Captain James Cook, upon seeing a man riding the waves in a canoe, wrote, "I could not help concluding that this man felt the most supreme pleasure while he was driven on so smoothly by the**

"Kahele and I watched the surf-swimming for some time, charmed with the spectacle." Engraving by Wallis Mackay, ca. 1873, Bishop Museum.

sea . . ." That Cook suffered a rather unpleasant fate at the hands of the Hawaiians did not deter Mark Twain from journeying to the Islands. With his uncanny ability to land a plumb gig, Twain secured an assignment as travel correspondent for the *Sacramento Union* after the Civil War. Traveling by outrigger canoe to the ancient ruins at Honaunau, an eight-mile journey round-trip, this wry observer of the human condition encountered an astonishing sight, which he duly recorded in *Roughing It:*

"In one place we came upon a large company of naked natives, of both sexes and all ages, amusing themselves with the national pastime of surf-bathing. Each heathen would paddle three or four hundred yards out to sea (taking a shortboard with him), then face the shore and wait for a particularly prodigious billow to come along; at the right moment he would fling his board upon its foamy crest and himself upon the board, and here he would come whizzing by like a bombshell! It did not seem that a lightning express train could shoot along at a more hairlifting speed."

Duke Kahanamoku with Jane Waite on his shoulders in the Waikiki surf, Oahu, Hawai'i, 1929, Bishop Museum. Photographer Warren Tong.

Twain arrived just in time to bear witness to this phenomenon, for the missionaries were also pouring into the islands to spread the Word and save souls. They took a dim view of surfing (naked or otherwise). They simply could not countenance this practice that was a kind of language itself, joyously hedonistic and as deeply rooted in the Hawaiian culture as music or dance; as such it was

Tandem surfing with Diamond Head in the background. Waikiki, Oahu, Hawai'i, ca. 1935, Bishop Museum.

anathema to the Calvinist virtues of hard work and productivity. Sheldon Dibble referred to the "evils resulting from all these sports and amusement," citing "the constant intermingling, without any restraint, of persons of both sexes and of all ages, at all times of the day and at all hours of the night."

Like the native language, which in an 1872 edict was forbidden to be taught in the schools, surfing all but disappeared from Hawaiian life. In defense of the missionaries, Hiram Bingham argued that "the decline and discontinuance of the use of the surfboard, as civilization advances, may be accounted for by the increase in modesty, industry and religion." It could also be accounted for, in part, by the decimation of the native population by diseases such as smallpox, for which they had no natural immunities. **By the 1890s, with the language nearly extinct and the native population reduced to a mere fraction of precontact numbers, surfboards had become museum pieces, relics of a pagan past.**

Hawaiians would eventually find their way back to surfing, for the sea and the waves and the riding of the waves were in their blood—even Twain, having made his own ill-fated attempt to catch a wave, admitted that "none but natives ever master the art of surf-bathing thoroughly." In 1911, **Duke Kahanamoku**, then the world's best-known surfer, cofounded the Hui Nalu (Hawaiian words for "gathering" and "surf") Surf Club, the Hawaiians' answer to the Outrigger Canoe Club. While the members of the club were almost exclusively *haoles* (whites), some of them not terribly athletic, membership in Hui Nalu was by election only, and to join this elite group, you had to possess some athletic ability. The Hui Nalu Club included two of the islands' best female surfers: **Mildred "Ladybird" Turner** and **Josephine "Jo" Pratt.** Considered the best woman surfer in the Islands in 1910, Pratt surfed Canoe and Queens off Waikiki.

Tandem surfing, in which two or more surfers rode on a single board, was an attention-getting device that yielded some historical footnotes for women's surfing. Duke surfed in tandem with **Leslie Lemon**, who stood on his shoulders, and also three on a board with **Marion** and **Beatrice Dowsett**, riding the length of the surf break at Canoe. Duke became a kind of goodwill ambassador for the sport, traveling around the world to give demonstrations. In 1914, he gave a three-hour surfing demonstration at Freshwater Beach in Australia, using a seventy-five-pound board made from a plank of sugar pine by a local builder whose fifteen-year-old daughter, **Isabel Letham**, was in front, watching the exhibition. For the finale, Duke wanted a young woman to surf in tandem with him, and Isabel, who excelled in rough-water swimming, was plucked from the chorus. "When we caught a wave, I was terrified," she recalled. "It was like going off a cliff." After her ride, she was hooked: "It was the most thrilling sport of all," she exclaimed. She rode with Duke at a second exhibition and was later inducted into the Australian Surfing Hall of Fame.

Thanks in part to Duke's goodwill ambassadorship, surfing found a second home in Southern California in the 1920s. One of Duke's California disciples was Mission Beach lifeguard **Charles Wright** who in turn found his own willing pupil in the form of **Faye Baird Fraser**. They rode tandem at first on a thirteen-foot redwood board imported from Hawai'i, but Fraser was game to try it by herself—even though she was one of only a handful of surfers out there, and none of them were women. "But oh it was wonderful," she recalled in a 1987 issue of *San Diego Magazine*. "You could look down and there was water, all around you. You had to really concentrate." One

Shirley Temple with mother and surfboard. Honolulu, Oahu, 1935, Bishop Museum.

time she caught a wave in Pacific Beach, north of Mission Beach, and rode it all the way to shore at Crystal Pier. On New Year's Day, Belmont Park had just opened, and she and Wright put on a demonstration for the crowds: "We caught three waves in total darkness. The only way we could see where we were going was by lighting several waterproof flares. The water was so cold I could hardly stand it, but even so, I can't recall having more fun."

For most, braving cold and dark on a surfboard would not be the idea of a fabulous New Year's celebration. The notion of warm water and palm trees seemed a more tempting proposition. Hawai'i had become an irresistible allure to sun-worshiping tourists from the mainland, and by the 1920s and '30s, Waikiki had been discovered as a tourist destination. In 1927, the Royal Hawaiian Hotel opened, awash in the same patina of celebrity pink as the Beverly Hills Hotel.

Hollywood celebrities were especially enamored of Waikiki as a tropical getaway. In 1935, seven-year-old child film star Shirley Temple made a trip to Honolulu, where she was named honorary captain in the Waikiki Beach Patrol and presented with a special surfboard inscribed "Aloha Capt. Shirley." She performed her hit song "On the Good Ship Lollipop" from the second-floor balcony of the Iolani Palace to throngs of adoring fans. Sadly, there is no record of her actually trying out her new board on the pillow-soft breaks off Waikiki. What a pity, to be deprived of this unscripted moment, little Curly Top clambering up on her board and that familiar voice exclaiming, "Oh, my goodness," as she tumbled off her board into the surf.

In 1939, another Californian, **Mary Ann Hawkins**, arrived in Honolulu to compete in the 1939 Duke Kahanamoku Swim Meet. A swimmer who at age seventeen won the AAU 500-meter freestyle title, Hawkins was cut in the mold of an Esther Williams. However, in 1934, her family moved from Pasadena to Costa Mesa so that she could train in the ocean, but Hawkins discovered a new calling. "I fell so in love with surfing and bodysurfing," Hawkins said. "I never really did my best in swimming from that time on." She became the premier women's surfer in California, winning virtually every contest. In Honolulu, she broke the Hawaiian 200-meter freestyle, and like others before her, she paid homage to the reigning king of the sport by surfing with Duke at Waikiki.

Back on the mainland, Hawkins used her glamorous looks and facility in the water to get work as a Hollywood stunt double. She stood in for such stars as Dorothy Lamour, Shirley Jones and Lana Turner. On ABC's *You Asked for It*, she set a world record for holding her breath underwater for two minutes and fifteen seconds. In 1956, she found herself back in Honolulu, paired with Esther Williams in a water show at the Hilton Hawaiian Village. She used the success of the show to launch a successful swim school, teaching an estimated ten thousand people to swim.

Hawkins also continued to surf until 1983, when her son drowned while working in Alaska. Her first inclination was to use surfing as a way of reclaiming her son. "I felt that if I got out in the water again, maybe I would be closer to him and closer to God," she said. It was quite the opposite: a solitary experience that only served to heighten her feeling of loss. She never surfed again.

For these early pioneers, surfing was like going off a cliff, a kind of freefall that brought exhilaration and joy. Surfing with the great Duke Kahanamoku. Shooting the pier on New Year's Eve. But it proved a tangential kind of joy. They performed but did not compete; they experienced its beauty and sheer exhilaration, but when they looked to it for solace, or as a means of finding God, they found it wanting.

Today these early women of the waves would undoubt-edly have gone on to have great professional careers or opened surfing schools or taken on the big waves. But for them, the boards were too heavy, the opportunities too few. They showed it could be done, that it was possible.

And soon, a new wave of surfers was to arrive on Hawai'i's shores, Californians who dreamed of being the best in the world. To prove your worth, you did not catch waves in pretty-in-pink Waikiki; you went to a place called Makaha. ✳

CHAPTER 3

Tandem surfers at Makaha International Surfing
Championship, Oahu, Hawai'i, ca. 1960, Bishop
Museum. Photographer Laurence Hata.

MAKAHA

MAKAHA
IS HAWAIIAN FOR "FIERCE."
ONLY THIRTY MILES FROM WAIKIKI, ON THE
WESTERN, OR LEEWARD, SHORE OF OAHU,
IT IS AN INHOSPITABLE PLACE. THERE
ARE NO PINK HOTELS, NO BEACH BOYS
NOR UMBRELLA DRINKS. There are just a series
of interconnected surf breaks, a beach and a broad reef. In summer, the waves are four feet or below; however, in winter, the waves are indeed fierce, rolling in as high as fifteen feet. Makaha can be as tricky as it gets—you take off in the Bowl into a steep drop, which leads into a section called the Blowhole. If you hit the Inside Reef just right, you're in the tube; if not, you discover how Makaha got its name.

In 1937, only two years after Shirley Temple knocked 'em dead at the Palace, two Waikiki surfers, **John Kelly** and **Wally Froiseth**, decamped to Makaha to escape the tourists and test themselves on the surf break. A crude village of Quonset huts sprang up and became home to the surfers who encamped there in winter.

Testosterone remained the unofficial hormone of Makaha until the 1950s, when the Makaha International Surfing Championships were held. In 1953, the first contest was scheduled, but there were no waves, a pointed reminder that nature is in charge. Without the diversion of competition, boredom set in and tempers flared, first between the Makaha and Waikiki surfers and then between the Hawaiians and the Californians who had come over to partake in the competition. There were even heated disagreements over how to roast the pig for the *lū'au*.

The following year, 1954, nature proved more cooperative, and the first competition took place. There was no women's division, but **Joanie Jones** rode in tandem with **Walter Hoffman** to win the tandem division. **In 1955, the women had their own division, and, fittingly, the winner for the next two years was Ethel Kukea, a Californian who had married into a Hawaiian surfing family and thus could be considered a local.** A forty-year-old YWCA fitness instructor and mother of three, Kukea had begun surfing in Corona del Mar in the 1930s with her older brother, **Lorrin "Whitey" Harrison**, a pioneering surfer who was still riding the waves in his eighties. Perhaps, as Twain remarked, no one can surf bathe as well as the natives, but Kukea, with her Hawaiian pedigree and graceful style, came close.

Among the competitors in 1958 was a thirty-two-year-old California mother of two, Marge Calhoun. Her arrival in Oahu, less heralded than that of Shirley Temple, had an immediate and profound effect on her personally. "When the door of the airplane opened and the warm, fragrant air hit me, I realized I hadn't known anything like that existed," she said.

Calhoun had come to surfing relatively late in life. Born in Hollywood, the daughter of a set designer, she seemed destined to follow the same career track as **Esther Williams**. Like Williams, she trained to compete in swimming in the 1940 Olympics, which were canceled because of World War II. She then did stunt work for the movies and performed in synchronized swimming routines at Marineland, an aquarium/theme park on the Palos Verdes Peninsula.

It was her husband, Tom, who recognized that she had potential to do more than perform stunts with trained whales. In the mid-1950s, they were watching surfers at the beach at Topanga, just north of Santa Monica, and he turned to his wife and said, "Marge, you could do that." For Christmas, he gave her a surfboard—not your traditional stocking stuffer, a bitch to wrap, but a gift that would last her a lifetime. She took her new board down to the Malibu Colony, where she ran into **Darrylin Zanuck**, daughter of producer Darryl Zanuck. **Zanuck became the surfing mentor for Calhoun, who proved to be a quick study, and by 1958, she was ready to face the challenge of Makaha.**

In Hawai'i, she and her friend **Eve Fletcher** rented a panel truck for $100 a month from Fred Van Dyke, a big-wave surfer from the North Shore. This truck was to be their home for the next month. **For the competition, she rode a ten-foot balsawood board made by Dale Velzy, one of the leading surfboard shapers of his era. She finished first in the women's division, establishing herself as one of the world's top women surfers.**

The following year, Calhoun faced competition from another Californian. Diminutive (only 5'2") and shy, **Linda Benson** was only fifteen, and she did not possess a Hollywood or performance background. She grew up in Encinitas, just north of San Diego, and learned to surf at Moonlight Beach on a battered 8'6" balsawood board that her father had purchased for $20. In 1958, at age fourteen, she saw a story about Calhoun winning at Makaha, and she cut out the picture of her new idol and hung it on her bedroom wall for inspiration. That year, Benson won the first U.S. Championships, held in Huntington Beach; then, in that determined style that would become one of her trademarks, she launched her campaign to compete in Makaha.

Linda Benson, San Onofre, California.

It was one thing for Calhoun to compete. She was thirty-one, a mature adult. But the notion that a fifteen-year-old girl would travel three thousand miles across the Pacific to compete in a place where the lingo was rough and the waves sometimes rougher seemed, in that day, inconceivable. But Benson was not to be denied this chance to compete against the world's best. The proud possessor of a new Dale Velzy foam board, her prize for winning at Huntington, she approached the veteran shaper and asked if she could join the group, then all-male, that he took each year to Hawai'i to compete at Makaha. Velzy agreed to send her if she could pay her way back to California. Benson induced her father to foot the bill for the return trip, and thus she became the young-est person ever to compete at Makaha.

Huntington Beach Surfing Walk of Fame.

In Hawai'i, Benson was entrusted to the care of Hobie Alter, founder of Hobie Surfboards, and his wife, Sharon. She stayed with the Alters on the North Shore and surfed every day with her Hawaiian competitors. The day of the contest, her heart in her throat, she paddled out on a nine-foot foam board into the five-footers at Makaha. A goofyfooter (a surfer who rides the board with a right-foot-forward stance), **Benson caught the judges' eyes with her hot-dogging style.** She modeled her style after that of **Dewey Weber**, himself a small surfer (only 5'3") who developed a flamboyant style involving quick turns and other trick maneuvers. Recalled **Mike Doyle**, who saw Benson that day at Makaha, "She had incredible wave judgment and literally ripped the waves apart." **Benson was the new female world champion.**

Following their triumphs at Makaha, both Benson and Calhoun found their appetites whetted for surfing the big waves of the North Shore. Calhoun surfed the breaks from Haleiwa to Sunset. "I was a big, strong woman," she said, "and I was always good in big surf. I loved the takeoff and that drop down the face of a big wave. It was so exhilarating."

Waimea, whose intimidating winter surf had turned back many a male surfer, had yet to be surfed by a woman. *Waimea* means "reddish," a result of the combination of mud and silt, but one surfer who felt the wrath of a big-set wave said, "At Pipeline it's white when you're underwater, and at Sunset it's gray. Waimea is black." The dark heart of this surf break made itself felt in 1943, when one male surfer drowned and the other turned up on the beach unconscious. After that incident, the waves pretty much had the run of the place until 1957, when **Greg Noll**, known as "the Bull" for his size and head-down charging style, led a group of seven fellow lunatics out to test themselves in this death trap. They emerged in one piece.

In 1959, Benson decided to put herself to the same test. That day, the waves were running about eighteen feet, but height was only one of the difficulties facing Benson—the waves form into a near-vertical drop and are known to "jack up," or suddenly steepen. To catch the wave and make the drop at exactly the right moment is a matter of timing, speed and nerve—three attributes of which Benson was in no short supply.

But this was Waimea.

John Severson, founder of *Surfer* magazine, was on the shore taking pictures, and he told Benson, "You're crazy." Undeterred, Benson borrowed a ten-foot "gun," a longer, streamlined board used for big-wave surfing, and paddled out. A prudent person would have paddled right back to shore after watching **Fred Van Dyke** wipe out, his board sawed in half by the force of the waves—a sign that the surf was in no trifling mood. But Benson stayed out there, waiting nearly two hours for the perfect wave. How many times did she urge herself to take off: "Go, Linda, go!" And then the wave was gone, it was too late. Whether from a final gathering of nerve, the synapses all firing together, or sheer exhaustion, she finally went after a fifteen-footer. "I felt the drop and hoped I could stay on," she recalled. "I can remember the steepness, the speed of the wave and the spray of the water in my face from the wind. It nearly blinds you."

She emerged, unblinded, her person and her board both still intact, and she vowed never to surf Waimea again. But the experience of competing at Makaha, and getting her first taste of freedom, had an indelible effect on the fifteen-year-old. "I was on my own," she said, "but everyone took care of me. It was a time of real innocence and joy."

For Calhoun, too, Makaha was a transforming experience. "I quickly realized that I was with people who feel like I do. They just adore the sea. I like their lore, everything about the Hawaiians." She brought her daughters, Candy and Robin, with her in 1962 and again in 1963, when all three competed at Makaha. The surfing Calhouns' honey-golden hair and tanned skin moved Mike Doyle to describe them as "Greek goddesses."

They weren't goddesses, at least not in the sense of mythical figures like Venus on the half shell, emerging full-blown from the sea, invested with divine powers, pushed ashore by mythical winds. **These were flesh-and-blood women, and they had to paddle out and claim their place in the waves. They were not in it for the money, which was fortunate, as there was none. Nor for the fame, although** Linda Benson **was greeted by a small entourage at the San Diego airport when she returned to the mainland.** But there were no sponsors lining up with nifty togs and endorsement checks; they had to find their own way to pursue their passion. Calhoun and her daughters surfed together, becoming a fixture at Southern California contests and hot surfing spots. **Surfing formed an indelible bond between mother and daughters.**

Benson went on to win five U.S. championships, but to earn a living, she became an airline attendant, working the L.A.-to-Honolulu run for United. The crew stayed in a small hotel a couple of blocks from Waikiki Beach, and Benson kept her board in a locker so that the minute she arrived, she could hit the waves. Sometimes she would stay out surfing until they were fueling up the plane at Honolulu Airport—"Six feet at Queens, and I hated to leave!"—and she'd reluctantly drag herself from the surf to make her flight. How could this plane full of strangers heading back to the mainland have known that this petite blonde with the pixie haircut who was serving them coffee and tea had won Makaha at age fifteen, that she had surfed the big waves at Waimea?

HOW TO BE A REGULAR GIRL

The first-time former world champion **Mike Doyle** saw **Margo Godfrey** surf at La Jolla Shores, he said to himself, "There's the future women's champion."

His words proved prophetic. In 1968, at age fifteen, Godfrey beat out Joyce Hoffman **and the rest of the field to win at Makaha. Later that year, the ninth-grader, taking time out from algebra and English lit to compete, won the World Surfing Championships, held in Puerto Rico.** "She rode like a guy and was the first in my mind to be better than most of the guys," Doyle said, paying her what then was considered the highest possible praise.

At a young age, Godfrey had set out a plan for herself: "I'm going to surf 'til I'm sixteen, and then I'm going to be a regular girl." Now, however, she had the burden of success to carry, this fierce desire to compete versus the teenager's equally intense need to be liked, to fit in. In 1970, she lost her title to Sharron Weber and returned to Santa Barbara High in California to live through a miserable junior and senior year. "People kept asking, 'What happened, why didn't you win?'

Margo Godfrey Oberg.

The loss was so devastating that I retired." **Washed up at seventeen, a surfing prodigy who had appeared, ever so briefly, upon the world stage, then wiped out.**

In 1972, she married Steve Oberg, a Pentacostal pastor from San Diego, and moved to Kauai. **The least developed and commercialized of the Islands, this idyllic haven was the ideal place to surf and raise your family and be the normal girl that you always wanted to be.**

It didn't happen quite this way for Oberg. Perhaps living in Hawai'i, communing with the spirit of Duke and those early Hawaiian surfers, worked its magic upon her soul. Perhaps she felt a rekindling of competitive fire, a need to banish a lingering high school humiliation. With a new crouching style that emphasized function over form, Oberg returned to the mainland in 1975 and won the Women's International Professional Surfing Championships in Malibu for $1,000, a sum that would just cover expenses. After losing to Lynne Boyer in 1978, she took a year off (now a characteristic pattern), then returned to capture the world titles in 1980 and 1981. She finished third in 1982, but she could be forgiven this lapse in form, given that she had given birth to her first child three months before.

Oberg struggled with wanting to be a good and proper Christian and wanting to have a good time. "The rowdy in me wants to dance," she said. "The other side wants to go to church." When it came to religion and surfing, however, there was no ambivalence. **"Surfing is a way of humbling ourselves before God and praising Him for such an abundant life," she said.**

Humility before the Lord was one thing, but humility before the rest of the world sometimes eluded Oberg. When asked who her favorite surfer was, Oberg, in all modesty, replied, "Probably me." She once described herself as "the woman's Gerry Lopez," a reference to the sinewy, graceful tube rider who was named the ninth most influential surfer of the century by *Surfer* magazine. Oberg herself had become an accomplished big-wave rider, naming Sunset as her favorite break. "It was scary," she said, "and I never got sick of it. I never even got close to what I really wanted to do on a Sunset wave."

In 1992, Oberg found herself in a final heat with Wendy Botha, a South African surfer. A perfect wave came along, and she and Botha were both positioned to catch it. For once, Oberg, who had a reputation as a wave hog, did not go for it. Instead, she paddled into the channel and gave the wave to Botha. It was at that moment that she realized her pro career was over. "Before, I had a real hunger for everyone to say I was the best. Then I realized I didn't care anymore." The Lord giveth and the Lord taketh away; Oberg took, and then she gave away. It was not so much the spirit of giving, but a loss of desire to compete.

Freed from the demands, both physical and psychological, of competition, Oberg could devote her time to her surfing school, which she had been operating on Poipu Beach on Kauai since 1977. **As for her dream of being a "regular girl," she had been too consumed with being the best for that to have been possible.**

"I was going to be a normal girl," she said. "But it never happened, and now I'm glad about it." ✳

Inspiration: Rell Sunn

The Lord giveth, and the Lord taketh away. He raises from the sea the pure spirit of surfing and breathes it into a young Hawaiian girl. She is of the ocean, and lives in it and through it, and knows the pure joy of riding the waves; and then, for reasons of His own, He takes that spirit and commits it back to the sea.

Rell Sunn must have known in the womb that she would become a surfer. Her family lived at Makaha, on Oahu's leeward shore, when it was still relatively wild and remote, and surely, bobbing on that warm sea inside her mother's womb, she could hear the song of the waves calling to her. Did she sense, even then, that one day she would be called the Queen of Makaha? Did she know that her biggest battle would be, not against the waves or her fellow surfers, but against a much tougher opponent?

Born in 1950, Rell Sunn was raised in a Quonset hut with her four siblings, and instead of a teddy bear, she would sometimes sleep with a surfboard in her bed, reaching over to run a hand along the rail, the edge of the board. "Can you imagine being four and knowing what love is?" she said.

Rell Sunn knew the ocean with that intimate knowledge of the Hawaiian born to the sea. She could read tides and wind and waves. She could dive and spear fish and paddle an outrigger. And she could surf. She had an excellent mentor in Richard "Buffalo" Keaulana, a naturally gifted surfer with a smooth fluid style and an uncanny instinct for being in the right place at the right time to catch a wave. In 1960, Buffalo caught all the right waves and won the men's division of Makaha. His Hawaiian approach to surfing—less aggressive and attacking than becoming one with the waves—influenced Rell, whom *Surfer* magazine anointed as the "supreme female stylist." She must have watched the likes of Linda Benson and Joyce Hoffman surfing at Makaha and winning trophies, and wondered at their skill, secretly knowing that she had a special affinity for the sea that was unmatched by any of them.

Having won the Hawaiian Junior Championships at age sixteen, Rell was invited to compete in the 1966 World Championships in San Diego. Two years later, she found herself, not in her natural ocean habitat, but becalmed on land. She had moved to Oklahoma with her boyfriend, married and had a child. The marriage didn't last; perhaps it was too much to expect that union to hold up against her abiding love of the sea.

In 1972, Rell returned to Makaha with her child and took up the surfing life. With the shortboards now in vogue, she became newly proficient and regularly was in the top group of women surfers, finishing number three in the world in 1979 and 1982.

Rell Sunn's career, which roughly paralleled that of Margo Oberg, seemed to embody the true spirit of the soul surfer. A term that is thrown about rather loosely to describe a surfer who was interested less in contests and winning than the pure joy of surfing for its own sake, it aptly described Rell Sunn, who surfed, not in the attacking style that was becoming popular among men and women in the '70s, but in that smooth, graceful style that was reminiscent of the old Hawaiians. The notion of the soul surfer also speaks to a kind of narcissism that is surfing's dark undercurrent; Rell Sunn was anything but narcissistic.

While others were frantically competing, she became the first full-time lifeguard in Hawai'i. In 1976, she got her B.A. in anthropology from the University of Hawai'i—giving lie to the notion that surfers are willfully ignorant of anything but surfing. She also taught hula and hosted a radio show, where she displayed an impish, very Hawaiian sense of humor. One day, she reported that the waves at Makaha were running six feet, really rolling—but the surf in fact was flat that day. Momi Keanulau, Buffalo's wife, asked her, "Were you lonely that day?" "Exactly!" Rell replied.

In 1977, she founded the Rell Sunn Menehune Contest in Makaha, which attracted young boys and girls into surfing. Megan Abubo, who would later become one of the world's top female surfers, competed in the Menehune as a youngster. "I first met Rell when I was ten," she recalled. "She gave me some of the best advice I've ever heard from anyone. Her attitude, her outlook on life, her respect for the ocean, should be spread throughout the world."

The Gospel According to Rell was spreading around the world, through young surfers whom she sponsored to attend the surfing contest in Biarritz, France, and through her membership on the board of the Surfrider Foundation, which is dedicated to preserving the ocean environment that she loved so dearly.

SURFING WALK OF FAME
HUNTINGTON BEACH

Rell Sunn
Woman of the Year
1996

Above: Rell Sunn, floating. Photographer Dennis Oda.
Left: Huntington Beach Surfing Walk of Fame.

But in 1983, Rell suddenly found herself face to face with her own mortality when she was diagnosed with breast cancer. She endured every indignity that this devastating disease can visit upon a woman: chemotherapy, radiation, a mastectomy, even a bone marrow transplant. The battle was joined, and eventually the disease prevailed, but it was the spirit of Rell that ultimately triumphed. Through the fifteen-year ordeal, she maintained her optimism and humor and generosity. She continued to serve as a worldwide ambassador for surfing. She even made a trip to China in 1986 to promote the sport of surfing to the sons and daughters of Chairman Mao.

More than three thousand mourners turned out for her memorial service. Buffalo's son Brian had put out the word to the surfing world: "Bring sand from your beaches, water from your surf and a conch shell for the sound of a thousand blowing at once." **Dave Parmenter, her husband, Jan Sunn, her daughter and her brother Eric paddled out in Rell's canoe to the blow hole at Makaha, Rell's favorite lineup, and as they scattered her ashes over the sea, the mournful sound of one thousand conch shells rose up as one from the shore: the ocean had reclaimed one of its own.** ✳

CHAPTER 4

The heirs to Gidget catch waves
at Surfrider Beach in Malibu.

THE CHUMASH INDIANS CALLED IT HAMALIWU—

"THE SURF SOUNDS LOUDLY"

COMMON NAME MALIBU, THIS PLACE WHERE THE SURF SOUNDS LOUDLY WAS, IN THE WORDS OF SURF JOURNALIST PAUL GROSS, "THE EXACT SPOT ON EARTH WHERE ANCIENT SURFING BECAME MODERN SURFING." Malibu was endowed with all the necessary components to become the epicenter of a surfing revolution: it had Surfrider, the near-flawless point break north of the Malibu Pier, where the waves form into a long, gorgeous continuum. It had **Mickey Dora**, "the black knight of surfing," and the rest of the errant knights who surfed Malibu in the 1950s and created their own surfing mystique. It had board designers **Joe Quigg** and **Mike Doyle**, whose innovations were to radically transform the ancient sport of kings. **And it had Hollywood. The stars who took up residence in the exclusive Malibu Colony, just north of Surfrider, lent an aura of glamour to this California beach town.**

Norma Jean Baker, who was to metamorphose into the tragic persona of Marilyn Monroe, was not only beautiful, she was athletic, and in the 1940s she tandem-surfed with **Tommy Zahn**, the legendary surfer and paddleboard racer from Santa Monica. Zahn, who remembers her as "tremendously fit," recalled, "I used to take her surfing up

Malibu, California

at Malibu . . . in the dead of winter, when it was cold, and it didn't faze her in the least; she lay in the cold water, waiting for the waves. She was very good in the water, very robust, so healthy, a really fine attitude toward life."

Zahn dated **Darrylin Zanuck**, daughter of studio head **Darryl Zanuck**. Something of a surfing buff herself, Darrylin commissioned Joe Quigg to create a surfboard for her. **The existing surfboard design called for a redwood-balsa plank that was tree trunk heavy and about as maneuverable. Quigg fashioned a balsa board covered in fiberglass and resin that was light as a feather and, equally important, fit into the back of Ms. Zanuck's Chrysler convertible. "She was really the first girl to buy a surfboard and buy a convertible and stick the surfboard in the back and drive up to Malibu and drive up and down the coast and learn to surf," Quigg recalled. He dubbed the board the Easy Rider, but it has gone down in history as the Darrylin.** Three years later, Quigg fashioned a similar board for **Vicki Flaxman**, another of the "Malibu surf girls" of the 1950s. This 9'6" board was so light and responsive that by the end of the summer, Vicki was, Quigg acknowledged, "surfing better than most of the men."

GIRL/MIDGET/GIDGET

**Sixteen-year-old Kathy Kohner riding a wave, 1957.
Photo © Allan Grant, Time Life Pictures, Getty Images.**

Then there was Gidget. Born from the dreams and longings of a fifteen-year-old girl looking for a place to belong, Gidget became a worldwide phenomenon who, depending on whose revisionist history is being read, is either a proto-feminist icon of women's surfing or a scourge who ruined Malibu for all time.

It was the summer of 1956, and every weekend, fifteen-year-old **Kathy Kohner** went out to the beach in Malibu—better to be outside in the fresh air, her mother said, than in a dark movie theater. She became part of this group of guys who hung out at the Pit at Surfrider and spent their days waiting for waves. They weren't quite sure what to make of this girl who had suddenly materialized among them.

"She's a girl." "She's a midget." "She's a gidget!"

They had names like Moondoggie and Misto and Tubesteak, and they had their own lingo: the waves were bitchen, and they were jazzed, and they said "tough shit" a lot and "Jesus Christ," but not the "f" word—that had not yet crept into the vocabulary.

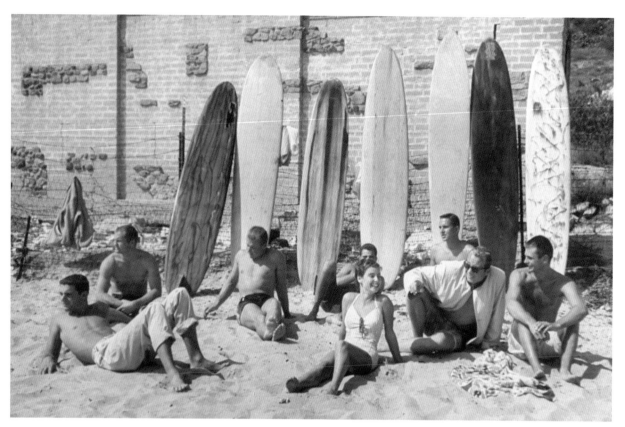

Kathy and the gang at Surfrider, 1957. Photo © Allan Grant, Time Life Pictures, Getty Images.

Kohner bought her own board from **Mike Doyle** for $35, and she paddled out and watched and learned and caught her own waves—and in between, she had crushes and dreamed the dreams of fifteen-year-old girls—and then the surf would beckon, and she'd go back out.

The boys threw everything they had at her—the language, the unmerciful teasing, the faux hostility. They buried her surfboard in the sand; they stole the distributor cap to her car. If she left them alone, it still wasn't enough. "You're still breathing, aren't you?" **But they underestimated this Gidget. She was no princess poser from Brentwood. She loved them and their life, and she loved the waves. She brought them peanut butter and radish sandwiches, and gradually she stole her way into their hearts.**

In 1958, she wrote in her diary, "I am now part of the group." And what a group it was—"a circumference of men" is how she now describes it—but they were boys, really, living the dream of the endless summer in Malibu. And she was living it with them. In Malibu, in their rough company, she felt at home, she felt that she belonged.

One day, she announced to her father that she wanted to write a book about her experiences. Frederick Kohner received a PhD in Vienna and, in 1936, fled Germany. He ended up in California, where he wrote screenplays for Columbia and the other major studios. On weekends he visited the Malibu Colony, Hollywood's beach enclave, but he could not have imagined the parallel-universe

Gidget inspired a generation of female surfers.

Malibu that his daughter inhabited. Fascinated by the stories she would tell him, he offered to write a book based on her experiences, and so they became collaborators, the German-born father and this California girl; the manuscript was completed in six weeks.

On Thanksgiving, a call came from Kohner's agent. "You want to go on that ski trip to Europe? Well, now you can." It wasn't just a book—there would be a movie and a TV show and even comic books. Kathy, the girl, became Gidget, the teenage surfer girl, and Gidget became a household word around the world, an indelible emblem of the California surf culture.

The endless summer finally ended, and it was time to put away childish things. Kathy went away to college at Oregon State; Gidget, her alter ego, continued to surf in the summer. Then came a long hiatus in which surfing was not a part of her life. She still had the original diaries, yellowed and aging, the covers falling off, and in those fragile pages were the even more fragile memories of youth: "Boy the surf was so bitchen today I couldn't believe it. I got some real good rides from inside."

In 2006, the fiftieth anniversary of Kathy Kohner's arrival on the surfing scene, there was a sudden resurgence of interest in the Gidget phenomenon. There was an article in *Vanity Fair* and another in the *Los Angeles Times*. Kathy Kohner (now Kathy Zuckerman) was in demand as a speaker for youth groups, seniors and even the Republicans. When asked her political affiliation, she diplomatically replied, "There are no politics in the water."

In 1999, *Surfer* magazine named her the seventh most influential surfer of the century.

Considering that she never competed or won a surfing championship, this measure of her influence might seem hyperbolic—until one considers the effect she had on women's surfing. Proto-feminist or not, she proved to millions of young girls that surfing was not gender-specific, that a girl could hold her own out in the waves. In the documentary *Accidental Icon*, they recall how seeing the movie or TV show inspired them, and how the nickname became a kind of badge of honor.

> Layne Beachley: "Gidget was my nickname. . . . If they looked for Layne, no one knew who they were talking about."

> Jericho Poppler: "She made girls realize they could do something that was considered just a man's thing."

Carla Rowland: "I loved the TV show. They called me little Gidget."

Rochelle Ballard: "You were the Gidget if you hung with the guys."

Kassia Meador: "She has the aloha spirit, she loves life."

Was Gidget a Proto-Feminist?

The surf today is filled with girls who were either inspired by Gidget or (if they're too young to have heard of her) have dozens of examples on which to pin their surfing dreams. Yet Kohner rejects the idea that she played a role in the gender wars, defying traditional notions of what girls could and could not do. "Back then, I didn't even know the word 'gender,'" she said. The only girl in a "circumference of men," she held her own, but she was not out in the world to challenge the guys or compete with them.

"People call me a proto-feminist," she said, bemused. "I don't even know what that is." When told that Linda Benson, a pioneer of women's surfing, was inspired by the *Gidget* book, she seemed at a loss for words; she was just a girl, hanging out with some guys, surfing—how could that be?

Rachel Wegert respectfully dissented. Having grown up watching the *Gidget* movies and TV shows, this student at Long Beach State decided to do her master's thesis on Gidget. Her premise: Gidget was a feminist icon who, without following either extreme of the feminism paradigm, helped to make surfing an acceptable choice for women.

Wegert's professor at Long Beach State was appalled at the idea: how trivial, how inconsequential. Go back, bring me the surfboard of the Wicked Wahine of the West. Undeterred, Wegert decided to up the ante. She had lots of feminist theory from which to draw, but the libraries were not filled with original source material about Gidget. She had the original *Gidget* book and started calling all the Kohners in the L.A. area. She finally reached Kohner's nephew, an

entertainment lawyer who, cautious at first, met with Wegert and ended up giving her his aunt's phone number. Now there was a real face and voice and life to attach to the myth.

Wegert ended up getting an A on the paper, though her professor never conceded that Gidget was a legitimate subject. She and Kohner are good friends, and she is close with her son and nephew. **She doesn't want to exploit Kohner's story, but she tells the story to all her students to encourage them to be uncompromising and, in particular for women, to follow Kohner's example and use cooperation rather than competition to achieve their goals.** "She had a genuine quality," she said. "She didn't compromise her personality."

Did Gidget Ruin Malibu?

When the first *Gidget* movie came out in the summer of 1959, a few of the guys from Malibu went into Santa Monica to see it. When they came out of the theater, Tubesteak **turned to his buddies and said, "This is the beginning of the end."**

Like a dark shape lurking under the water, the belief that Gidget somehow ruined Malibu for the surfers still floats to the surface. Pre-Gidget, so goes the argument, the surf belonged to the true aficionados who had carved out this hidden piece of paradise for themselves. Post-Gidget, everyone and his brother, it seemed, were buying boards and coming out to Malibu to have a go. The following year, 1960, there were as many as 250 surfing wannabes out on the surf line. "It went nuts," recalled **Dave Velzy**.

In 1995, **Fred Reiss** wrote a novel called *Gidget Must Die*, in which a surfer returns to Malibu to kill everyone in the *Gidget* movie as revenge for ruining his beloved surf spot.

Why hold Gidget responsible? Blame the advent of lightweight foam boards. Blame Hollywood. Blame the Beach Boys. **You can kill off Gidget metaphorically, but the real Gidget lives forever, not just in the movie and the book, but as part of surfing history.**

Gidget Redux

What of this Gidget, now a woman in her sixties? In the foreword to the 2001 rerelease of the *Gidget* book, "Now that Gidget is back—the real Gidget will be back, too. Who says sixty-year-old Gidgets can't ride the waves anymore?"

No one says it, at least not out loud, certainly not within earshot. How could this petite woman, who looks like she could be knocked over by a piece of Rye Krisp, possibly expect to surf again? In 1996, she had gone out with **Mike Doyle**, who had sold her her first surfboard and worked as a stunt double on the *Gidget* movie. Doyle got his old friend Gidget out into the water again, and by her own accounting, it was wonderful. But to go out again, ten years later, where the water is cold and the surf is loud and the other surfers look at you wondering what you're even doing out there in the surf lineup?

Never count out the Gidget. She was to ride the waves again, at the insistence of another surfing buddy who coaxed her into participating in the Legends of Longboards, a fund-raiser for the cancer center at Scripps in San Diego. So early on a Tuesday morning, she paddles out to First Break, not at all certain that this was a good idea. She's out in the water and she's a little scared, because it's not like riding a bicycle, it doesn't all come back to you at once, and she isn't sure she can spring up in that quick agile motion and adjust her feet; the water is in constant motion, its sole intent to upend her.

Then a shove of her board and a shout: "Come on, Gidget, you can do it!"

And on that day in Malibu, it was just like the ending of the novel, life imitating art fifty years later, the cries of "Shoot it, Gidget, shoot the curl!" And this tiny sixty-something woman, she gets up on that board, and this girl, this midget, this Gidget, she shoots the curl. *

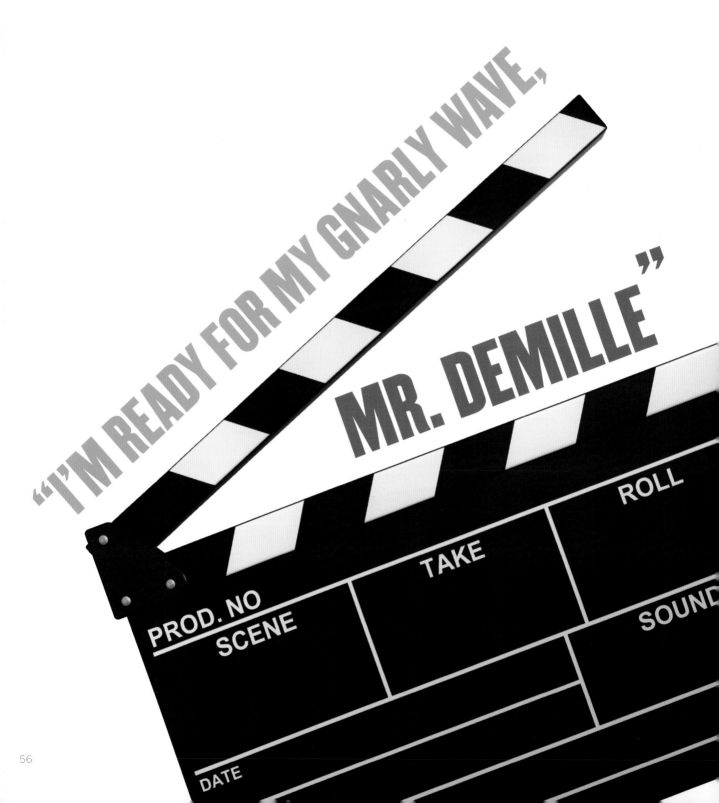

CHAPTER 5

"I'M READY FOR MY GNARLY WAVE, MR. DEMILLE"

Documentary filmmaker Elizabeth Pepin.

BEFORE THERE WAS *GIDGET* THE MOVIE, THERE WAS *GIDGET* THE NOVEL. *GIDGET* THE MOVIE WAS FOLLOWED BY MORE MOVIES AND THEN *GIDGET* THE TV SHOW. EACH ITERA-TION MOVED FARTHER AND FARTHER AWAY FROM THE ACTUAL GIRL WHO WAS THE ORIGINAL INSPIRATION FOR GIDGET. YET DESPITE THESE DEVIATIONS, EACH VERSION REACHED AN EVEN WIDER AUDIENCE AND HELPED TO KEEP THE GIDGET PHENOMENON ALIVE FOR A NEW GENERATION.

The original novel by **Frederick Kohner, Kathy Kohner**'s screenwriter father, captured the yearning of this fifteen-year-old girl to belong, to become accepted by these surfers; it was also about her coming of age and her emerging sexuality. The plot is relatively simple—Gidget wants to learn to surf and to be accepted by the crew, as she refers to the surfers who hung out in Malibu, and she develops a huge crush on Moondoggie. Determined to make him notice her, she attends a luau (an orgy, the guys called it, in a effort to dissuade her) and drinks beer and spends the night—chastely—in the arms of Cass, a.k.a. the Kahoona. **"It was shocking, feeling a man's body like that," she says. "At that moment I knew that I had never lived at all."** Moondoggie and the Kahoona end up in a fight, and at that moment, **Gidget grabs a surfboard and goes out, the guys yelling from the shore. She catches a wave and stands up. . . . "Shoot it, Gidget, shoot it!" she shouts to herself over the roar of the waves.**

Sally Field as Gidget from the 1960s TV series. Photo © Bettmann/CORBIS.

This final scene of the novel—this young girl alone in the surf catching her own wave—was pure Gidget—impulsive, headstrong, fiercely independent, full of life. Some critics saw Gidget as a female Holden Caulfield, shredding convention, setting the establishment on its ear. She does say "hell" and "damn-it" and "bitchen," and takes a wide-eyed view of this life of endless waves and no obligation. But if Gidget was Holden, she was a very lighthearted version of him. She has it over other intrepid teenage heroines—Jo March, Anne of Green Gables, Nancy Drew—she could exert her force of will, with feminine charm; oh, and one more thing—she could surf.

This novel must have just about killed Jack Kerouac. *Gidget* hit number seven on the *New York Times* best-seller list; Kerouac's beat classic *On the Road* was number eight. Gidget, perhaps more than Kerouac and his merry band, had resonated with younger readers; here was a book, light on its feet but speaking a new language: the language of youth. Gidget and her pals at the Pit were that to which all American youth, then and now, aspired: they were cool.

Columbia hired Paul Wendkos to direct the movie, based on Frederick Kohner's screenplay. He was less than thrilled to be handed this project, which he regarded as somewhat frivolous. In retrospect, he came to see it as a serious sociological shift, a connection with the youth culture that touched a deep nerve. "The concept of feminism being explored was fabulous," he said.

The film, which starred a comely unknown named Sandra Dee as Gidget, with Cliff Robertson as the Kahoona, is not exactly a feminist tract. While Gidget proclaims, in her ingenuous way, that "surfing is the ultimate!" she spends the first part of the movie making coffee and fetching burgers. She doesn't so much surf as flail in the water; she becomes entangled in a bed of kelp, and back on the shore, her makeup is perfect, every hair in place. When she finally does stand up on a board, it is clearly Sandra Dee in a studio, an unconvincing illusion of surfing. In the real surfing footage, **Mickey Muñoz** gamely served as her stunt double. In the second half of the film, her interest in surfing seems to wane, and she devotes most of her energy to setting a mantrap for Moondoggie. In the end, the Kahoona gets a job, Moondoggie decides to go to college, and the film ends with him and Gidget strolling on the beach in their party clothes. **The conventions of the 1950s—responsibility, ambition, conformity—have prevailed, and Gidget, that feisty free spirit who goes out and surfs at the end of the novel, is chastely back on the shore where she belongs.** Still, as Ben Marcus points out in *Surfing USA!* "At least she did more than hold her man's towel, wringing her hands with worry as her beau risked his neck in the heavies."

Following on the success of the first Gidget movie, Columbia cranked out *Gidget Goes Hawaiian*. In this version, Gidget is played by **Deborah Walley**, and her stunt double is none other than **Linda Benson**, the six-time U.S. champion. She and her fellow surfers laughed at the depiction of surfing but not at the money—the then-queenly sum of three hundred dollars a day.

An unknown teenager named Sally Field played Gidget in the original TV series. The beach scenes were shot in winter, when the water was numbingly cold. Still, Field remembers this as "one of the great, wonderful things of my life." Said Field, whose feisty personality more closely mirrored that of Kathy Kohner, "She will always be me. The Gidget is inside."

With Gidget thoroughly imbedded in popular culture, the image of women's surfing remained arrested in a 1950's fantasia of modest two-piece suits, boy-crazy capers and the occasional ride on the waves (managed with no hair out of place). In 2002, this dated image was swept away by a film called *Blue Crush*. **The heroine, Anne Marie, was played by actress Kate Bosworth, who is not a surfer but for the sake of her art put on fifteen pounds for the role. "I had so much fun . . . being at that body type," Bosworth confided in** *US* **magazine.** The screenplay, written by Lizzy Weiss, provides a tough, hard-edged take on the women's surfing scene. Anne Marie and her two gal pals live a hardscrabble existence, cleaning rooms at a posh Oahu resort so that they can surf. Her nemesis is her own fear: she wants to surf Pipeline, to prove something to herself and to the "assholes who think you can't surf Pipe because you don't have the balls." But she can't quite summon the nerve. She is egged on both by her friend, played by Michelle Rodriguez, who admonishes her to "stop being such a Barbie," and by one of the guys: "You came to surf Pipe," he taunts Anne Marie, who is, quite sensibly, surfing over by the sandbar. "This isn't Pipe." There is a love interest, a pro quarterback who provides a pleasant distraction from her goal. But after some cavorting in the surf, and a sleepover with the quarterback in a plush suite in the same hotel where she works, she gets back to business. In the climactic scene, Anne Marie is out in the surf lineup, paralyzed with fear, until Keala Kennelly paddles over to her and convinces her to go for it. She drops down into a perfectly formed tube and, with the help of stunt double Rochelle Ballard, surfs a beautiful run that scores a ten. It is a vintage sports cliché ending, but an eminently satisfying one, providing the viewer with a pulse-pounding adrenaline rush.

Heart of the Sea was an award-winning documentary about Rell Sunn.

Despite its obeisance to Hollywood movie conventions, *Blue Crush* managed to break new ground, depicting girls not as beach bunnies whose primary ambition is to get the guy but as tough and fearless, willing to hold their own in the surf lineup and to take their fair share of waves. The film had a similarly galvanizing effect as *Gidget:* girls who missed out on the Gidget phenomenon or failed to relate were suddenly encouraged to emulate these cool, gorgeous girls out there in the surf, riding the waves.

Having discovered a successful formula for female surfing films—a beautiful, plucky heroine, hunky male love interest, gorgeous beaches and some dynamite surfing footage—Hollywood was not about to plunge into the nether reaches of surf noir. That genre was the novelist's province, first explored in Kem Nunn's impressive 1984 literary debut, *Tapping the Source.*

This dark, edgy story of a teen boy who comes to Huntington Beach to search for his missing older sister earned it a nomination for an American Book Award. In an uncanny bit of prescience, the novel foreshadowed actual events; it was around the same time that **Lisa Andersen** ran away from her home in Florida to Huntington Beach to pursue her dream of becoming world surfing champion.

Nunn's next surf noir novel, *The Dogs of Winter*, came out in 1997, this time set in the chilly waters of Northern California. Noir now also had a female voice in **Joy Nicholson**, whose debut novel, *The Tribes of Palos Verdes*, came out the same year. A scathing Holden-like indictment of PV's cliques and shallow mores, the story is told through fourteen-year-old Medina Mason, who desperately seeks an escape from her family and the cruel "towel girls" ("they laugh, they point, they twitter"). "I'm going to be the only girl to surf Palos Verdes," she declares. Her father gives her an article about Frieda Zamba, the great Florida surfer. "'Don't limit yourself to being a lame chick in the water,' Zamba advises. 'Use your mind—and your arms.'" Medina cuts out a picture of Frieda and hangs it over her bed.

She practices with her brother, Jim, in the two-footers of summer and early fall and then takes on the big swells of winter, joining the Bay Boys in the surf line. During this odyssey, she discovers the sensuality of surfing. "It's a frank sexual pleasure to be wet and warm, lying alone on my stomach near the mouth of the sea, relaxing completely, then pushing my body upward while taming the liquid motion."

The book ends darkly with her parents divorced and Jim in a mental institution, where he takes an overdose of pills. She seeks solace in surfing. "I'm never lonely when I'm in the ocean—I talk to my brother when I surf." She returns to their old spot in Palos Verdes and rides her brother's board, and then shoves it against the breakwall, where it shatters into pieces. Soon she will be surfing in Hawai'i, then Bali, Java, Thailand. "I'm going to surf until I die."

This dark tale is in sharp contrast to the story of Summer, whose frenetic energy and relentlessly upbeat attitude make Gidget look like the angel of death. In *Surfer Girl,* the first in a series of teen novels, Summer swims competitively, surfs, eats vegetarian, hangs out with her friends, scopes out the boys (and she is highly selective, this Summer)—all that, and she still has time to save the environment. Her parents were hippies, but of the purest kind: they protested the war and ate organic but didn't do drugs or practice free love. Boyfriend number one gets the boot because he rides ATVs in the desert: "I think you can enjoy the desert," she admonishes him, "but I don't think you need to run rampant all over it," suggesting that he "become one with the desert like I become one with the ocean." Boyfriend number two, Philip, apparently not put off by Summer's smug self-righteousness, is enlisted in the midnight rescue of a baby seal that was injured in a gill net. "This is my legacy," she tells him. (Oh, to be fifteen and have a legacy!) The seal pup is rehabilitated and released back into the ocean, with Philip and Summer swimming alongside; one finds oneself yearning for the cheerful ingenuousness of Gidget or a bit of brooding noir to cleanse the palate of all this sanctimoniousness.

The stories of flesh-and-blood female surfers, as opposed to these soap dolls carved out of writers' imaginations, provide every bit as much drama and pathos. As a graduate student in film at Stanford, Charlotte Lagarde made a four-minute film called *Zeuf* about a woman who used surfing in her fight against breast cancer. Following that well-received debut, she made *Swell,* about four generations of women in Santa Cruz. Both films were less surf documentaries than they were intimate portraits of individual women living unique lives.

Having founded Swell Cinema, a nonprofit production company based in San Francisco, in 1996, Lagarde found herself inexorably drawn to the story of Rell Sunn, a Hawaiian surfing legend who succumbed to breast cancer. The subject had to be approached with some delicacy: Rell

is more than just an icon to the Hawaiians; she is the embodiment of the aloha spirit, and her memory is fiercely protected. This outsider suddenly materializes, this Swedish filmmaker, and they did not quite know what to make of her, but Charlotte Lagarde won their trust and was with Rell in her last days. The documentary *Heart of the Sea: Kapolioka'ehukai* (2002), a moving indelible portrait, transcended the usual surf genre tropes by exploring not just Rell's surfing career and her battle with cancer but her deep, almost spiritual relationship with the ocean. "Before I could read, I could read the ocean," Rell says. **She is also seen as an accomplished water woman who spearfished for her supper, as a single mother, as the "auntie" who organized surf contests and encouraged kids to stay out of gangs and off drugs, and as the woman who took a group of kids to surf in France and went to China as an ambassador for the sport.** The film won the PBS Independent Lens Audience Award 2003, the Audience Award at both the San Francisco International Film Festival and the Newport Beach Film Festival and Best Documentary Award at the Ashland Independent Film Festival.

Missing from the surf film genre was a road-trip movie. In 2004, that void was filled with *AKA: Girl Surfer*, a documentary directed by Todd Saunders. Along for the ride were six-time world champion Layne Beachley, Rochelle Ballard, Rebecca Woods, Belen Connelly, Karlee Mackie and Melanie Bartels—all on the pro tour or aspiring to join it. With surfboards in tow, the girls boarded a bus and headed down the Australian coast, hitting a different surf break every day. They surfed and played and frolicked, filling their off-hours lawn bowling, indoor bowling, even taking a trip to the zoo.

Beachley acted as unofficial spokesperson for the trip and a kind of roving ambassador for women's surfing. "Guys used to say, 'chicks can't surf,'" she said. "Well, we've proven that totally wrong. We're testing ourselves, expanding our abilities." Having watched the younger women and admiring their skill, she said, "Give a girl the opportunity and the time, and it will generate and bloom into something beautiful and something great."

More in the reflective spirit of Lagarde's films, Elizabeth Pepin, a producer at KQED-TV in San Francisco and the principal photographer for this book, and Sally Lundburg directed *One Winter Story,* a 2006 documentary about Sarah Gerhardt, the first woman to surf Maverick's. The documentary follows Gerhardt through four grueling seasons battling the punishing cold, fear and physical demands of surfing Maverick's. Like Lagarde's films, it does not traffic in such surf film clichés as the showdown contest or the big wave; instead it focuses on one woman seeking to balance the physical and spiritual demands of surfing, to push herself to new limits. It's not Hollywood, but it plays very well to those seeking an informed authentic view of women's surfing.

Also running counter to the Hollywood formula is *Heart of a Soul Surfer,* the 2006 documentary about Bethany Hamilton, who lost her arm to a shark while surfing off Kauai in 2003. First-time director Becky Baumgartner, who worked as an assistant to the family, produced the film in association with Walking on Water, an organization devoted to spreading the Christian message through surfing. The thirty-minute documentary portrays a young girl who loves surfing and whose deep-rooted faith saw her through her ordeal. "Jesus means everything to me," says this slight blonde girl with braces. The surfing footage, taken both before and after the accident, is a powerful testament to determination and will (enhanced with no small amount of natural athleticism); whatever one's religious leanings, watching this footage cannot help but convey a sense of hope and possibility for the future.

Who, then, should have the last word? Who should come out on stage for the final scene? Why, Gidget, of course, or rather, Kathy Kohner. In October 2006, at the Malibu Celebration of Film, all of Malibu, and some of Hollywood as well, turned out for the world premiere of *Accidental Icon,* billed as the true story of Gidget. This was no multiplex with a small screen and the smell of stale popcorn; it was Smothers Theater at Pepperdine University, filled to capacity. Gidget was back, both in the

one ordinary woman...
one extraordinary wave

one winter story
The inspirational life of big-wave pioneer and scientist Sarah Gerhardt

a documentary by
sally lundburg & elizabeth pepin

Sally Lundburg and Elizabeth Pepin (right), producers/directors of *One Winter Story,* Frank Film.

Kathy Kohner Zuckerman, Malibu, California, 2006.

flesh and on screen. Before the screening, Kathy Kohner, stylishly attired in a sleeveless dress and sandals (practically fancy dress attire in the surfing world) came on stage and thanked everyone who "helped me get back my stoke." Then the screen was filled with the Kathy Kohner of fifty years ago, in a bathing suit, carrying a surfboard. It was a weird sort of déjà vu; the scenes on the screen, the woman in the flesh who had been the inspiration for what was transpiring on the screen. The lines of fiction and fact are forever blurred despite the film's attempts to sort them out; but there is a poignant moment at the end, when Kohner appears on screen, walking along the beach in Malibu. "I feel very much at peace," she says, "I feel very much at home." She looks into the camera: "This is the final stop for the Gidge."

Kohner has come to the place that was truly her home more than any other, and if it is a final stop, then what better place, walking those same beaches where fifty years before, a young girl had gone surfing with some guys. They had caught some bitchen waves, and everything that came after sort of washes away, leaving those memories clean and intact.

Whether we surf or we wait on the shore, whether we write or make films, it is just as Sally Field said: "Gidget is inside us." ✳

Sally Lundburg (right), shooting at Maverick's. Shawn Alladio is driving the Jet Ski.

Q & A WITH FILM DIRECTOR CHARLOTTE LAGARDE

Q. You've made three films about female surfers—*Zeuf*, *Swell* and *Heart of the Sea*. Why this particular focus?

A. The films are more about women than surfing. They're about women dealing with challenges and overcoming them.

Q. The first was *Zeuf*. How did you come to make that film?

A. I was doing my master's at Stanford, and I met this ICU nurse who had had a mastectomy. I did a two-hour interview with her, which I spliced down to the essence of the story. Surfing helped her find herself.

Q. You compressed a lot into a short time.

A. It was four minutes. *Zeuf* is a haiku.

Q. Then you made *Swell*, another film about female surfers.

A. *Swell* was about a community of three generations of women surfers in Santa Cruz—one eight-year-old, three teens and a woman in her forties. It came out right before *Surfer Girl*. It was about cold-water surfing and the long board—"the lost tribes of the surfer"—or is it?

Film director Charlotte Lagarde.

Q. When you made *Heart of the Sea*, about Rell Sunn, the legendary Hawaiian surfer and water woman, Rell was in the final stages of her battle with cancer, was she not?

A. I saw this woman walking down Makaha Beach, this very thin, sick woman, and I thought, that can't be her, and then I said, "Holy shit, this is Rell." It was heartbreaking.

Q. Yet she was still able to go ahead with filming?

A. We spent ten days at Makaha, but the whole time we were there, we were on Rell time. If she

wasn't feeling well, she'd send us off to the Bishop Museum to look at the surfing exhibit.

Q. Was there any resistance from family and friends to your making this film?

A. Makaha is a very close community, and they considered Rell as one of their own. We went tide-pooling with her friends and became allies. Also we befriended her sisters through *Zeuf.*

Q. What is the focus of the film?

A. Rell didn't want it to be about her dying. So we made it a day in the life. It was about her being a surfer, a single woman and dealing with cancer.

Q. With her being so desperately ill, how were you able to make the film?

A. It was very challenging. I did a three-hour interview with her, which became the backbone of the film.

Q. What did you take away from your encounter with her?

A. Rell is an inspiration to all the people who met her. Do what you want, and don't take anything for granted.

Q. What do you like most—or least—about women's surfing?

A. I don't like the shredding. Rell's style was one of pure beauty—she was one with the ocean. Lisa Andersen did something fabulous—she was outspoken and beautiful, and she brought women's surfing to the attention of the national press.

Q. What's your take on some of the other female surfing films, *Blue Crush*, for example.

A. I couldn't care less about *Blue Crush. AKA: Girl Surfer* did much more. *Blue Crush* was an easy

CHAPTER 6

Emilia Perry, Jenny Useldinger, and Katherine Carter, North Shore, Oahu.

Surfing in Style

This particular occasion was a party held on the night before the finals of the Roxy Jam Longboard Championships at Cardiff Reef. One doesn't want to be overdressed, but on the other hand, one doesn't want to look like a piece of seaweed dredged up from the beach, so white jeans, a turquoise top and matching sandals, with turquoise earrings and bracelet: casual, beachy, but a notch up from flip-flops and shorts.

This outfit proved to be a fashion faux pas. The (mostly younger) female competitors turned up in jeans and tank tops and flip-flops; the few men were in jeans and Hawaiian shirts. White jeans and turquoise bling looked like they belonged on the Strip in Vegas, not at a surfing party at Cardiff Reef.

Surfing, like any subculture, has its own elaborate fashion codes, subtle dos and don'ts that are intuitively understood by insiders but easily misinterpreted by outsiders. Casual and practical are only the starting points; surf fashion takes off with its own special variations, developed through years of trial, error and striving for the ultimate definition of cool.

In the 1940s, Dale Velzy and the other surfers at the Manhattan Beach Surf Club cut off the legs of their white sailor pants just above the knees. Long and loose fitting, these trunks didn't fill up with water and protected the thighs from rubbing against the board. Along with their "baggies," the surfers also took to wearing huarache sandals, which were durable and cheap and the antithesis of the businessman's wing tips. Some took it a step further: in 1958, big-wave surfer Greg Noll showed up at Waimea Bay in a pair of black-and-white-striped jailhouse trunks that became his signature.

One of the original surfwear lines was Kanvas by Katin, founded by Nancy Katin. **Known as the "First Lady of Surfing," she and her husband** Walter Katin **opened Kanvas by Katin and by 1959 were producing a rugged line of surf trunks that proved a huge hit with surfers.** In the 1970s, Katin, a cheerful, diminutive maternal figure, was featured in ads surrounded by surfers wearing the company's line of surf trunks: Kapers, Kontenders and Eyekatchers. Kanvas by Katin sponsored the Katin Pro-Am Team Challenge from 1977 to 1998; only one year, 1987, featured a women's division, won by Lisa Andersen. Curiously, Katin, a revered figure who was inducted in the Surfing Walk of Fame in 2000, did not develop surfwear for women.

Over the years, establishing a fashion identity for female surfers has presented something of a conundrum: how to have comfort and practicality, to be surfer-casual and look feminine at the same time. Marge Calhoun, one of the pioneers of women's surfing, encouraged girls who took up surfing to retain their feminine identity in this aggressively masculine environment. "The boys didn't make the girls feel welcome in the water," she said, "so many of them felt they had to imitate the boys. I'd tell them that they didn't have to look like a gremmie, in baggy suits with uncombed hair."

Naked surfing having been ruled out by the missionaries and the bulky wool bathing costumes a relic of the past, a minimal standard was established: a snug-fitting suit and neatly combed hair.

It wasn't until the 1990s that the surfwear industry awakened to the enormous marketing opportunities presented by women's surfing. That year, Quiksilver, the Australian surfwear maker, started a women's line called Roxy. "Fun, Bold, Athletic, Daring and Classy" were the buzzwords coined in the company's annual report. The company put its heart on its sleeve with the Roxy logo, a heart-shaped crest adapted from the Quiksilver mark.

Roxy lays claim to a surf-fashion coup—the boardshort, a fashion-forward design that combined fit and flexibility with a more feminine styling. The boardshort, so the Roxy version goes, was developed in a brainstorming session with Roxy's fashion designers and Lisa Andersen, by then a sponsored member of the Roxy team.

Lane Davey, Hawai'i's amateur surf champion in 1994 and founder of Us Girls, insists emphatically that it was she who came up with the idea of a boardshort for women, a shorter cotton version of the male boardshort, adorned with flowers. "When I made the first women's boardshort in 1993, I could only dream that women's surfwear would really catch on," Davey says. Two years later, she modeled her boardshort in an advertisement for Water Girl, a women's surfwear shop, in *Wahine*

ESSENTIALS: THE WETSUIT

For surfers who venture out into cold water, subcutaneous fat is not enough to provide insulation from the cold. For the numbing chill of Maverick's and other breaks off the California coast, a wetsuit is de rigueur. **Brenda Scott Rogers**, the first female surfer-CEO, has made it her life's work to create high-quality wetsuits for male and female surfers. Winner of the 1978 World Cup at Sunset and named the World Tour Rookie of the Year, she and Japanese exporter Hiro Iida cofounded **Hotline Wetsuits** in 1979. For more than twenty-five years, the Santa Cruz–based company has created custom wetsuits for a broad range of sizes and body types.

With the burgeoning interest in surfing, many wetsuit makers have come on the scene, creating off-the-rack products made of neoprene, a stretchy, forgiving substance. "The sport is very mainstream," says Scott Rogers, "and has become homogenized by the bigger companies." Hotline, in contrast, pioneers cutting-edge suits that are known for their durability and quality. Tall and lanky, short and stocky—whatever your body type, Hotline can fit you like the proverbial glove.

Hotline has sponsored up-and-coming surfers and others who have carved their way into surfing history—**Sarah Gerhardt**, the first woman to surf Maverick's; **Kim Hamrock**, a.k.a. Danger Woman, who won the 2006 Pipeline contest; and **Jenny Useldinger**, a hard-charging big-wave surfer who also rides for Roxy. Scott Rogers herself still surfs, taking inspiration from older women surfers, and proud that at forty-nine she can serve as a role model for younger surfers: "Us old pros are still at it," she says.

Brenda Scott Rogers, Santa Cruz, California.

Daize Shayne is stylin' with a checker-board surfboard and a Billabong wetsuit.

magazine. The shorts appeared in local surf shops, under the name **Us Girls,** one of the few surfwear makers owned and run by a female athlete. She also created a "good bikini that stays on," with adjustable ties in back.

"We know what our customer wants, how she wants it to fit and how it has to function," says Davey. "We use real surfers, not models." Resentful of the male-dominated big companies that "took the whole industry out from under us," she is making bathing suits again, working with a big chain to market them. "It's a great stepping-stone," she says. "I prefer to deal with a bigger store that respects my skill."

The marketing of women's surfwear recognizes a basic retail verity: While boys go for the image and logo, girls are more interested in style and fit. "**Andy Irons** wins a competition wearing his signature board short, and all the boys go out and buy that short because they want to be like Andy, but I think girls shop differently," says Holly Beck. "If you make a **Layne Beachley** signature whatever, maybe a couple people would buy it, but most girls are going to buy what fits or looks best, not what logo they like the most."

Tim Baker, an Australian surf journalist, sardonically noted that most of the actual gains have been "in women's shopping, rather than women's surfing." The surfwear giants—Roxy, Billabong, Rip Curl, OP, O'Neill, BodyGlove—have expanded from bikinis, boardshorts and wetsuits into sportswear, denim, shoes, jewelry, eyewear, even fragrances and linens. **By 2006, global retail sales for surfwear had reached $7.48 billion, the women's lines accounting for $327 million in surfwear apparel, according to the Surf industry Manufacturers Association.**

Not everyone in the surfwear industry is enamored of the mass-market, "bigger-is-better" ethos. **Donna von Hoesslin** is the owner/designer of a Ventura-based company called Betty Belts, a playful, alliterative reference to the "beach bettys"—girls who sit on the beach and watch their boyfriends surf. The belts and jewelry are handmade with natural materials such as cowrie shells, mother of pearl, abalone, glass beads, wood and stones. In 2006, Betty Belts, which prides itself on a green-is-good ethos, earned the Green Wave Award, given out by the *Surfer's Path* magazine for excellence and achievement in promoting environmental consciousness in the surfing world.

Von Hoesslin is a purist when it comes to making surfwear. "I wanted to support women who are really into surfing and not just buying into the look," she says. **"I'm adamant about supporting women's surfing. As small as my company is, I found the dollars to do that, get my girls in the ads."**

Von Hoesslin and others believe that the surfwear industry isn't doing enough to support women's surfing, that the money isn't going to the athletes; the ad dollars are going into ads in the mainstream fashion magazines, not grassroots surf magazines. "It's ridiculous," says von Hoesslin.

Lack of media exposure may be partly to blame. In the sports section of the *Los Angeles Times*, which surely would qualify as the "paper of record" for women's surfing, you can find the results for everything from lacrosse to water polo to beach volleyball, but women's surfing creates barely a ripple, not even on the last page. In 2005, Rip Curl International spent $600,000 to stage the Rip Curl Malibu Pro, but there was very little media coverage. "It was like banging

A QUIVER OF HER OWN

Julie Cox with one of her boards.

Most pro surfers have several surfboards, a "quiver" of boards for different surf conditions and styles of performance. "I like having a quiver of boards," says pro surfer Julie Cox, "A log, a high-performance longboard, an all-around longboard, a fish—I think it's fun to surf all kinds of boards." Working with Jed Noll, she brought out the Jule Collection, which includes the diamond model, the emerald, the sapphire, the ruby and the opal. "It's really feminine, but not teenybopper, hopefully— more for women in their 20s, 30s, 40s, 50s, 60s . . . 70s, 80s, 90s . . . kinda elegant, hopefully classy, really high-quality boards." In designing her boards, Cox listened to the comments of her female surf students—how their bodies are, how they like to surf. She incorporated their feedback with the dimensions and shapes that she finds work well.

your head against a wall," said Neil Ridgeway, the company's director of global marketing.

Media exposure for women's surfing has improved with the advent of Fuel TV, which broadcasts surf contests, and companies such as Roxy, Rip Curl, Op, O'Neill and Billabong are upping the ante for women's contests. The level of women's surfing continues to rise, giving it more legitimacy and attracting more media attention and financial backing. Men are even showing interest in the women's contests, gathering on the beach to cheer on their favorites.

But in the end, it is about the shopping. A girl from a suburb north of Los Angeles came into a surf shop in Encinitas. Her surf bona fides were discussed by the two sales clerks: "She's from Thousand Oaks," sniffed one of the clerks. "Total poser," the other agreed. But in fact, it is the posers—the nonsurfers—who buy the flip-flops and tank tops and crop pants and hoodies with the fur trim; they wouldn't know Layne Beachley from Santa Monica Beach; they may have never attempted to surf, but they know retail, for it is at the center of their existence. **On this simple primal desire rests the future of the industry. The small companies may inveigh against the crass commercialism, the compromising of surfing's purity, but it is upon the posers, the young girls from Thousand Oaks with their Visas and Mastercards, their insatiable craving to be cool, upon which the financial success of female surfing rests.** *

Peggi Oki, *Late Drop.*

PEGGY OKI: LATE DROP

About the Artist

Peggy Oki has combined her love of surfing with a passionate devotion to nature and artistic expression. A surfer for more than thirty years, Oki is an art instructor at Santa Barbara City College Continuing Education and youth art programs through the Carpinteria Valley Arts Council who has had more than twenty-one woman shows and fifty group exhibitions in the Santa Barbara area. Her love of surfing and travel and her commitment to saving the whales has taken her around the globe, from Hawai'i, Australia, New Zealand, Indonesia and Fiji to Mexico, Costa Rica and South Africa.

Artist's Statement

"Making art is a great visual and soulful expression combined with the physical experience of painting. Whether in my studio or outdoors in a natural setting, these passions complement each other, and my attention is shared between them to create a balance that I liken to the natural subjects that inspire me.

"I am in awe to see such radical surfers expanding the limits of surfing."

CASEY O'CONNELL: FALLIN

Casey O'Connell, *Fallin*.

About the Artist

Casey O'Connell grew up in Gainesville, Florida, not widely considered a surfing mecca. Nevertheless, she developed a passion for riding the waves. Today, this surfer and artist lives in a studio at Ocean Beach in San Francisco—an amenable balance between nature and city life. Casey approaches her art with beauty and grace. In her work, which exhibits a beautiful frailty, figures are often alone but resolute in their solitude. Her work has been featured in numerous publications, including the *New York Times, San Francisco Chronicle* and *Surf Life for Women*. Her work, which radiates a quiet energy, has been shown in Los Angeles, San Francisco, Seattle, New York City and Australia.

Artist's Statement

"When I was young I used to wake my mom up at dawn and beg her to go to the beach with me. I was just learning to surf and I wanted to be in the water as much as possible, but I was still a little scared of being out there. My mom would sit with me on the beach until I worked up the nerve to paddle out. Then she would watch as I tried to catch a wave. Hours would go by, and she would just drink her coffee and wave. I don't know how she did it, but when I finally caught something she would always see it and start cheering. She made me feel like a queen in knee-high slop. Those mornings are still the best sessions I have ever had."

Inspiration: On Being Bethany Hamilton

The Hawaiians call it *mako*—shark. This relentless, cold-blooded predator, numbering roughly 370 species and ranging in length from six inches to forty feet, prowls the waters of the earth. Some feed on plankton or other plant life, but most prefer some type of flesh.

They do not have a particular taste for human flesh; rather, they mistake humans for their regular prey.

By some unwritten code, surfers profess an indifference to the possibility of being attacked by a shark. The trick is to outthink the sharks, avoiding the times and places where they tend to lurk—e.g., dawn, dusk, popular feeding spots such as seal colonies.

The surfers are, to a degree, whistling in the dark. Shark attacks on surfers are a reality—in the twentieth century, according to the *Surfing Encyclopedia*, there were 441 recorded shark attacks, about two dozen of which resulted in fatalities. More than half of the attacks are from great white sharks, which still enjoy a gory reputation from the 1973 Steven Spielberg movie *Jaws*. But other sharks, while lacking in the size and girth of the jaw of the great white, can prove just as lethal.

On Halloween 2003, on the North Shore of Kauai, where there had never been a recorded shark attack, a fourteen-pound tiger shark saw something blue and shiny out of the corner of its eye. It swam toward the shiny object and discovered that this eye-catching bauble—a watch—was attached to the wrist of a thirteen-year-old girl, who was stretched out upon a surfboard, waiting for a wave. The shark, a bottom-feeder who has been known to eat anything, even tin cans, must have marveled at its good fortune—O succulent flesh, O tender morsel!

Bethany Hamilton didn't see the large gray fin closing in on her, or the drawn-back leer, the jagged teeth serrated like a steak knife. All she saw was the blur of gray, then red of her own blood in the water.

The wound was a clean cut just below the shoulder, but the mouths of scavengers such as tiger sharks are teeming with bacteria, so it had to be thoroughly cleansed. The surgeon then cut the nerves to reduce the potential for phantom pain, the sensation in a limb that is no longer there. In the second surgery, a flap of skin was removed from under her armpit and grafted across the open wound, providing a covering of natural skin over the stub. There was a transfusion, because her body was not replacing her own blood supply quickly enough.

The list of what you cannot do is very short, the doctors told Bethany; the list of what you can do is long.

But will I be able to surf again? she wondered. *Will I able to do the thing that I love best?*

Bethany's fellow surfers did not wait on the Lord to avenge this attack on one of their own. Laird Hamilton, the world's best big-wave surfer (and no relation to Bethany, other than being a fellow surfer and Hawaiian), put in a phone call to his father, Bill Hamilton. "If you don't go out and catch that fucking shark, I will." Ten days later, Bill and his friend Ralph Young went out in the waters off Kauai's North Shore, and they captured a fourteen-foot female tiger shark. The contents of its stomach did not contain the arm, nor the shiny blue watch—those would have passed long ago. But the jaws, those were a perfect forensic match to

Bethany Hamilton, Kona, Hawai'i.

the wound. This was the one. The skin of the shark was presented to a *kahuna*, or priest, to fashion a drum. Bethany asked for the teeth to make a necklace.

A nervous governor, anxious to put an end to this talk of sharks and its dampening effect on the tourist trade, declared the matter closed.

There is a beach in Kilauea, a secret place off the beaten path on Kauai's North Shore. On the day before Thanksgiving, Bethany walked down to the surf with her friend Alana. "It felt so good to step into the liquid warmth and taste the salty water that swept over me," she wrote in *Soul Surfer*, her recounting of the experience. "It was like coming back home after a long, long trip."

Using a longboard, she paddled out into the "soup," the white-water residue from the waves. It was like learning to surf all over again, without the benefit of a left arm. Instead of grabbing the rail, as you would normally do, she had to figure out how to brace her right hand flat on the center of the deck and get to her feet.

She felt the wave under her, pushed up with the one hand and was standing. The doubts vanished in the foam of that wave, and salt tears of joy spilled into the sea foam. She rode wave after wave, mostly white water, but she was back doing the thing that she loved. The next day, Thanksgiving, she went back out.

No soup for her on this day; she went out to the blue water, and on this day of thanks, she feasted on wave after wave, partaking of the bounty that the Lord had provided.

Over the next three years, Bethany Hamilton became a household word. She was named the ESPY Comeback Athlete of the Year and won the Teen Choice Award for Most Courageous Teen in 2004. She appeared on *Oprah* and *Ellen*. She released a perfume line—Stoked & Wired. She did a Volvo commercial. She spoke at the Crystal Cathedral and other churches. Everyone, it seemed, wanted a piece of her.

And she competed in surf contests. The girl with one arm outsurfed the dual-appendaged competition to win the 2005 NSSA National Championships. She won her first pro contest, the O'Neill Island Girl Junior Pro. Her surfing prowess impressed even the most jaded observers. "Straight up, Bethany Hamilton is a phenomenon," wrote Ben Marcus in *Wet* magazine. "What she is doing is scarcely to be credited, but she is doing it. With one arm and a supernatural will." Added photographer Jim Russi, "As I watched her paddling out through the lineup without missing a beat, I did not see a girl with a loss. What I saw was a complete young woman with faith, confidence and an amazing ability."

On a bright, hot November day in 2006 on Oahu's North Shore, Bethany is waiting for the other contestants for the Op Pro Haleiwa to get underway. With her blonde hair and braces, she has the look of an All-American teenager. Only at a second glance do you realize that something is missing. Her yellow rash shirt forms a kind of capped sleeve over the stump, which extends just beyond the shoulder.

Finally, the contest is underway. Bethany tucks her board under her arm and trots down to the water. With powerful strokes of her arm, she paddles out to the lineup. The waves are small but fast moving, and there is a tricky crosswind. She surfs well, holds her own—but she does not win her heat.

The Bethany who emerges from the surf is frowning. You want to go to her, to say, "You just did what most of us with two arms can't do." You want to tell her, "Hey, no one was surfing that great today; Layne Beachley wasn't surfing that great." But there is a wall around Bethany, a protective shield that she is not ready to let down. Perhaps she has had her fill of being the shark girl and reliving her nightmare over and over; perhaps, like that shark, everyone wants a piece of her. Or maybe the strains of trying to come to terms with losing a part of herself have begun to catch up with her. There is a kind of terrible bravery in this, to be among all these young girls whole and intact. As Bethany herself wistfully admitted in *Heart of a Soul Surfer,* the 2006 film about her experience, "All these beautiful girls with perfect bodies . . . " Yet she maintains that the experience has been a positive one, providing her with the opportunity to tell the world about God, to give people hope. "I had a choice," Bethany said, "to follow God or give up on life."

Even if she never becomes world-surfing champion, Bethany Hamilton will have done what few would have done— go back into the water, to face her fears, to emerge with her faith strengthened. ✳

Bethany Hamilton, NSAA Contest, Girls Semi-Finals, Kona, Hawai'i, 2006.

CHAPTER 7

She Who Surfs
BETTER THAN THOU

ONE UNSEASONABLY WARM DAY IN EARLY NOVEMBER, **LISA ANDERSEN** WAS OUT SURFING AT HUNTINGTON. THE SURF LINE WAS CROWDED WITH MOSTLY GUYS, AND IT WAS THE USUAL STORY: WHAT'S THIS CHICK DOING OUT HERE? JUST STAY OUT OF OUR WAY.

You can't wear a T-shirt saying, "Don't you know who I am?" That would be unseemly, as would a T-shirt proclaiming, "Lisa Andersen, Four-Time World Champion." You can't wear it or say it or scream it (even if you want to)—you can only show it out there on the waves. There was one guy who simply could not countenance this girl (though hardly that—in her mid-30s, she had lived three lifetimes) in their midst. Lisa saw him, and she saw a wave, and she paddled for it. Then another wave came, and she wanted it badly, and she took off—the guy dropping back. **His "Whoa, oh shit" spoke volumes, filling the heart of this former champion with gladness. She still had the chops; now he would not mess with her.**

Obviously the poor fellow was not a subscriber to *Surfer* magazine in the mid-'90s. Otherwise, he might have recognized this thirty-year-old with the blonde-brown streaked hair and fit physique who blasted onto the surfing scene with the force of a tsunami, prompting *Surfer* magazine to taunt its largely male readership with a cover blurb that read: "Lisa Andersen Surfs Better Than You."

Lisa Andersen at the Roxy Jam, Cardiff Reef, California, 2006.

Above and below: Lisa Andersen free surfing, Roxy Jam, Cardiff Reef, California, 2006.

By all rights, she should have been on a milk carton or dead at seventeen: "The body of a girl was found today in an alley . . ." There must have been a surf angel watching over her, one that saw under the toughness and the anger and somehow saved her from herself. She went from troubled teen to pro surfer to single mom to the most dominant figure in women's surfing in the 1990s.

For Andersen, surfing was an escape, a place where there was no drinking and fighting. Her parents disapproved—in their minds, surfing was synonymous with drugs, beach bums and no doubt that mother-my-god rock 'n' roll music. One day her father dragged her surfboard into the living room and jumped on it, breaking the fin. (**Linda Benson**'s father bought his daughter a board, **Marge Calhoun**'s husband gave her one for Christmas, but this dad broke his daughter's surfboard.) **Andersen left a note on the kitchen counter—"I'm leaving to become the world champion of women's surfing." She didn't know if there was such a thing as the world-surfing champion, but she cleaned out her bank account and bought a one-way ticket to L.A.**

She ended up in Huntington Beach, the self-proclaimed Surf City USA, where, according to the mythology that grew up around her, she slept on the beach under the pier. (It wasn't the pier, she later clarified. It was a bench in Newport.) It was there that her surf angel assumed the corporeal form of **Ian Cairns**, founder of the ASP. **It was Cairns who found her asleep under a table, and although she did not qualify to compete, given that she wasn't attending school at the time, he bent the rules and let her in. A brilliant, albeit brief, amateur career was launched.**

Andersen turned pro at age seventeen, and just as suddenly as it had materialized, this early brilliance flamed out. She made it through the early heats of competitions but folded as she went one-on-one with the other surfers. She place second in six finals, but the championship eluded her.

"I would rant and rave and punch things," Andersen now recalls. She finally realized it was not the board's fault, that to lose with grace makes a world of difference. "You don't have to show the whole world you're a loser."

Which came first: Roxy or the egg? "I was the egg," Andersen says. "Roxy hatched me." **Roxy, which had launched its line of women's surfwear in 1992, signed Andersen as its first team member in 1994. She had her first championship—and a daughter.**

Even in utero, little Erica proved to have a galvanizing effect on her mother's career. When Erica was born, her mother discovered a new resolve. "I had this enormous amount of strength that came after giving birth to Erica," she said. "Childbirth is not fun, but it's the most womanly thing you can ever experience and then, afterwards, you're invincible."

She cut herself off from all encumbrances, including her husband, whom she divorced. "I can't have a husband or a boyfriend or anyone telling me what to do," she said.

By the mid-1990s, the blonde, smiling visage of Lisa Andersen was everywhere: in magazine ads, on posters, in promotional videos. Some of the other female pros were understandably bitter over Lisa's growing celebrity. **"Women's surfing right now is Lisa Andersen,"** said former world champion Pauline Menczer. **"The rest of us might as well not even be here."**

Then came the proclamation on the cover of *Surfer* magazine, one that sent a powerful ripple of consternation through the male surfing community.

"Lisa Andersen Surfs Better Than You."

Who's this Lisa Andersen? wondered the members of the all-male surf club. *No way does she surf better than me.* "I was a little bit worried," Andersen now admits. "I'm not a cocky person. I didn't know how my dude friends would react."

They took it, and they liked it.

As a sign that she had truly transcended into the realm of mega-stardom, Andersen had her own stalker. "It was a kind of Fatal Attraction thing," she said of the French journalist who became

Pauline Menczer was ASP World Champion in 1993.

obsessed with her when she was in Biarritz and sent her postcards and romantic notes. He didn't stop there, however. "He sent me videotapes of me on the beach," she recalls. "Not shots of me surfing, but just hanging out, walking alone, sitting in the sand. It was creepy."

Andersen's career—and to some degree, her celebrity—abruptly ended in 1998 when she suffered a herniated disc. She attempted to mount a comeback in 2000 and finished fifth; in 2003, however, she failed to qualify.

It turned out she was not invincible after all, but she did achieve her dream of winning the world-surfing championship, not once but four times. **She was the only female, other than Gidget, to be listed as one of *Surfer* magazine's twenty-five most influential surfers of the twentieth century.** Ian Cairns' faith in her was vindicated. "Lisa's by far the best woman surfer in the world—whether she's winning contests or not," Cairns said. "She's one of a very few women who have total credibility among her peers, women and men."

Aspiring Lisa Andersens head out for the Roxy Jam.

Big-wave surfer **Rochelle Ballard** acknowledged Andersen's influence. "When you surf with Lisa, you find yourself smoothing out your own surfing. Her technique is so refined that it rubs off on everybody around her."

In the 2006 Surfer Poll Awards, bestowed by *Surfer* magazine on the world's best, Andersen came in third among the female surfers. "I was blown away," Andersen admits. "I was high as a kite that night. It was a huge confidence thing for me." Then comes the morning, and the next morning, and she is back at Quiksilver headquarters, giving advice and counsel, picking out the future champions from the crowded field of young female surfers.

"I should go to Vegas," Andersen jokes, "I know how to pick 'em"—and indeed she does. She saw **Chelsea Georgeson** surfing in Australia and told the Roxy team manager to get her a Quiksilver wetsuit. In 2005, Georgeson became the first woman to win the trifecta of the Vans Triple Crown, the Billabong Pro and the World Championship. **Sofia Mulanovich** was this "tiny little grom," but Andersen recognized the fire inside—"you could feel the energy," she said. She told Roxy to scoop her up, and in 2006 this "tiny grom" was the number-one selection in the Surfer Poll. Though she bested her mentor in the standings, Mulanovich was quick to acknowledge that "none of us girls would even be here today if it weren't for Lisa. She definitely opened the door for us. Because of her I've been able to accomplish more than I ever thought possible."

Andersen mentors her young charges, building their self-esteem, imparting the lessons that she learned on the tour: don't let losing get to you, don't let yourself be distracted by boys. In the obverse of her own childhood, she sees girls of thirteen and fourteen being pushed by their mothers, their childhoods being taken from them, and this troubles her. Erica, who turned thirteen in 2006, does not share her mother's passion for surfing. Andersen does not push it (perhaps remembering the note that she left and dreading the same). "I don't want her to think I don't love her," she says.

If you want to see if this mature, maternal Lisa Andersen still has the fire inside, simply mention Layne Beachley. "Layne is so driven, so competitive," she says of the Australian who won a seventh world championship in 2006. "It's like she has something to prove." As she walks down the hall at the Quiksilver headquarters, she pauses, considering her rival's championships, and how things might have been different if she had been out there competing with her. "It would have been a lot harder for her," she insists. On the wall is a giant poster of Kelly Slater, who won an unprecedented eighth world championship in 2006. "That'll keep him one ahead of Layne," Andersen says, with some satisfaction.

Andersen, whose autobiography was published by Chronicle Books in 2007, has enjoyed fame and success. Now she wants to give back by developing young talent and by her involvement with Joyful Heart. Founded in 2002 by Mariska Hargitay, the star of the long-running TV series Law and Order SVU, this foundation helps survivors of sexual assault heal in mind, body and spirit. The healing power of the ocean is a central part of Joyful Heart's approach. In a retreat at Kona, on the Big Island of Hawai'i, participants swim with dolphins and take surf lessons.

But the thing Andersen loves most is the thing she has not been doing. "I experienced the best times of my life through surfing," she says. "Surfing is art on waves, a form of self-expression." And since her injury, this has been virtually gone from her life.

She did some stand-up paddle surfing, which was a new way to rediscover surfing, and provided a different view of the ocean, even the world. She surfed with the legends at the Roxy Jam at Cardiff. Then there was that Sunday at Huntington, when she showed the "pig dudes" a thing or two. She loved being back in the water, with the wetsuit and the sand and the wet towels. "I felt like a little kid," she says.

She dreams of being out on a boat, no phones, the breeze in her face. "The saltier the better," says She Who Surfs Better Than Thou. ✳

CHAPTER 8

Where the Sun RISES OUT OF THE WATER

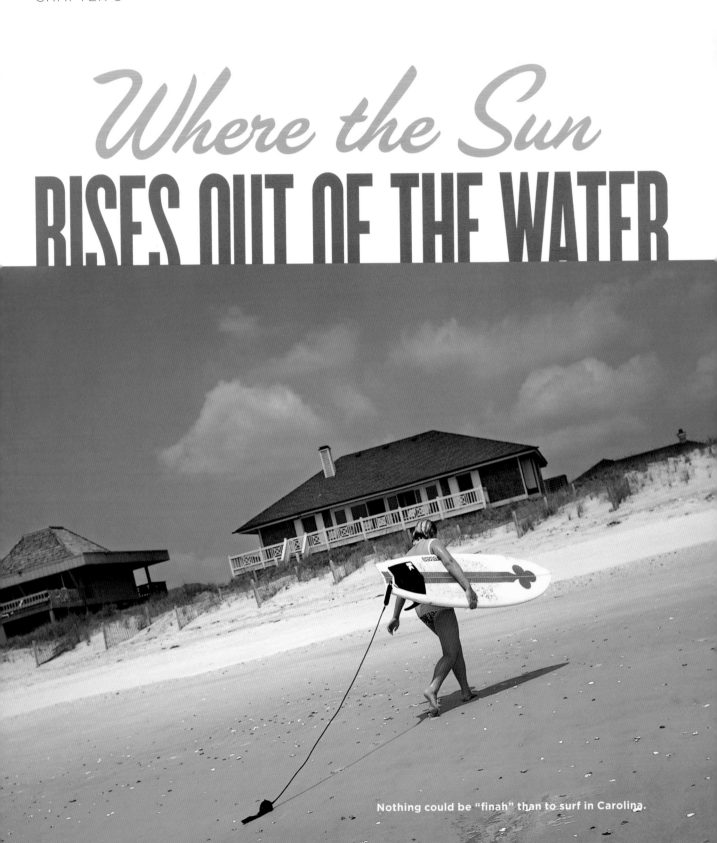

Nothing could be "finah" than to surf in Carolina.

Surf's up!

THIS IS MERELY ONE OF THE ANOMALIES OF THE EAST COAST—WHY DOESN'T THE SUN SET IN THE WATER, LIKE A PROPER WEST COAST SUN? THEN THERE'S THE OCEAN ITSELF— THE SURF BREAKS ALONG THE ATLANTIC ARE THE UGLY BETTYS OF SURF, WEAK AND ERRATIC. ALSO, THEIR PUBLICIST SHOULD BE FIRED: THEY DON'T HAVE A SONG WRITTEN ABOUT THEM, AND THEY DON'T HAVE NAMES THAT STRIKE FEAR AND AWE INTO THE HEARTS OF SURFERS.

So how is it that the East Coast has produced some of the world's greatest surfers, perhaps the greatest ever? The preternaturally gifted **Kelly Slater**, who became an eight-time men's world champion in 2006 (but who's counting), doesn't hail from California or Hawai'i, but from Cocoa Beach, Florida. **Lisa Andersen**, who grew up in Ormond Beach, was the perfect storm, a category five, a harmonic convergence of talent and will and heart who blew out of the Sunshine State and swept away everything in her path.

The answer is twofold: (1) Greatness will out, always. Give Isaac Stern a rusty saw, and he'll make it sound like a Stradivarius. Put Baryshnikov in cement boots, and he'll dance like he's floating on a cloud and (2) Bad surf makes for a good teacher. When the waves are small and unpredictable, you are forced to develop patience and the ability to make the most of what you are given.

While California and Hawai'i hogged what little spotlight there was on women's surfing, two surfing prodigies made the most of what they were given, emerging from the obscurity of the Florida surf to carve their names in the annals of the professional ranks.

Mimi Munro thought of herself as a grain of sand on the beach. She didn't take the surfing world by storm, but her quick feet and excellent balance made her one of the most skillful nose riders—and the East Coast Surfing Champion in 1965 and 1966; that same year, the fourteen-year-old finished third in the World Championships at Makaha. **Then the storm blew itself out, and she stopped surfing.** But her hiatus was not to last long. Her daughter took up surfing, and Munro began to dream of surfing, and she found herself out in the lineup, surfing better in her forties than she did in her youth. Indeed, the grain of sand was inducted into the East Coast Surf Legends Hall of Fame in 1966; ten years later, she won the East Coast Surfing Association's Goddess long-board and took second in the shortboard.

Maybe not Frieda Zamba, but pretty good!

There was this other Floridian who should have had a dance named after her: the Zamba. It should have become a worldwide craze. Instead, Frieda Zamba happened upon the competitive stage only to redact her interest in trophies and titles. Lean and sinewy, the hyper-fit Ormond Beach native won the Mazda Women's Pro in 1982; in 1984, at age nineteen, she became the youngest ever to win a world title. In 1988, after winning her fourth title, she retired from the pro tour and returned to Flagler Beach to open a surf shop with husband and coach Flea Shaw. She doesn't have a dance

The East Coast surf attracts surfers of all ages!

named for her (which is a shame, because it would have caught fire and been a great form of exercise); instead, the Zamba is among a line of custom surfboards that she designs. Says Zamba of herself and her fellow Floridians: "Florida surfers can make a terrible wave look good, just because we ride a lot of junk surf and adapt to conditions more easily than, say, a surfer from Hawai'i." That said, she still can be seen surfing the "junk" and making it look good.

That an injury shortened her brilliant trajectory into the surfing stratosphere doesn't diminish the influence of Lisa Andersen on women's surfing (See chapter 7: "She Who Surfs Better Than Thou"). Now the Roxy Global Brand representative, she is searching out young talent, trying to find among the "groms" the next Lisa Andersen. "The level of talent in women's surfing today blows my mind," says the former world champion.

To wit: **Connie Arias** and **Christa Alves**—respectively, "Cackle" and "Little Rocket." They earned these nicknames on the 2004 U.S. Surf Team that took the silver medal. Arias, a Melbourne Beach native who, in her Billabong bio, admits to a laugh being her favorite sound, had the last laugh by winning the 2007 Corona Extra Pro Surf Circuit Domes Event at Playa Domes in Puerto Rico. Alves, who planned to turn pro after graduation in 2007, has won nearly every contest on the East Coast, including the East Coast Surfing Championships, a midsummer pro-am contest held at Virginia Beach and the second-longest-running continual surf event in the United States. "Christa just gets it," said Brian Broom, competition director for the ESA. "She has a passion for competition and really knows how to score points. Her stature and dynamic personality will go far. She lights up the whole beach."

Alves and Arias will have to reckon with **Karina Petroni**, who worked her way to number one in the World Qualifying Series in 2006 at age eighteen, when she captured the O'Neill Women's Pro. Born in the American Zone of the Panama Canal, she moved to Atlantic Beach, Florida, at

age twelve and became the youngest ever to capture three amateur titles, including the Eastern Surf Association Championship. Poised to join the WCT, she has already tested herself on surf breaks from Puerto Rico to Indonesia.

But nothing could be "finah" than to surf in Carolina—at least in the opinion of surf journalist Nick Carroll, who likens the Outer Banks to Oahu's North Shore or the Gold Coast of Queensland. Known as "the graveyard of the Atlantic" for the hundreds of ships that have gone down in these treacherous waters, the Outer Banks draw surfers to the three- to six-foot sets that, during hurricane season, have been known to double or triple in size. Since 1971, the Eastern Surf Association Championships—"The Easterns"—as they are known, have become something of an institution on Cape Hatteras, a proving ground for young hopefuls who want to establish their surf cred and for more seasoned surfers who can still tear it up. In 2006, Jo Pickett took first place in Easterns in the Senior Women's division, and daughter Leilani won the Junior Women's title, the first mother-daughter duo to win at the Easterns. A mother of three who runs a surf camp in the summer, Jo Pickett also won the Goddess Shortboard and One Design fish divisions in the 10th Annual East Coast Wahine Championships at Crystal Pier in Wrightsville Beach, her home break.

Headed by Anne Beasley Weber, the East Coast Wahines have been surfing together for ten years, their numbers growing, their bonds strengthening. Says Weber, "More and more of us are finding solace and strength in the water, and an exceptional few are finding it is more than just a passion but a career choice with travel benefits." Predicting that "eventually the line between the girls and the boys abilities will blur," she adds this audacious prediction: "Since women are natural nurturers, we will be drawn to the plight of our ailing oceans and together we will use our energy to heal the planet."

Weber and the other wahines embody the spirit of that small group of women who, ten years ago, gathered on the beach to pay tribute, embodying the spirit of female surfers around the world, regardless of whether the sun rises or sets in the water:

"We wrapped Hawaiian ti leaves with shells and stones and asked the Queen of Makaha to bring us waves. A circle of women, from Maine to Florida in a sunset ceremony. And we were blessed. Aloha spirit spread quickly amongst East Coast surfer girls. We made new friends, saw old ones. We surfed. We laughed, we cried. We turned pink and then red in the sun. Our parched lips begged for more water. We celebrated womanhood, sharing our souls on incoming waves and changing tides." *

Waiting, waiting . . . now go!

CHAPTER 9

HUNTINGTON BEACH

IN THEIR 1960S HIT, "SURF CITY," JAN AND DEAN SANG OF THIS MYTHICAL PLACE WHERE "THEY'RE EITHER OUT SURFING, OR THEY GOT A PARTY GOING." HUNTINGTON BEACH, GENERALLY UNDERSTOOD TO BE THE INSPIRATION FOR THE TUNE, HAS LONG BEEN THE EPICENTER OF CALIFORNIA SURF CULTURE. Along its nine-mile stretch of coast, two-way breaks form consistently year-round, with larger ocean swells in winter. The pier has been battered by winter storms but still sports its familiar red cupola, a rallying point for hordes of visitors who descend in the summer.

Downtown Huntington is the home of the International Surfing Museum and the Surfing Walk of Fame, and in amongst the Starbucks and condominiums that have crept into the downtown area, there are still the surf shops and burger joints with surfing pictures on the wall.

Huntington struggles against a reputation as a kind of surf ghetto. In his surf noir novel, *Tapping the Source*, **Kem Nunn** describes Huntington as "hard, flat, colorless . . . squatting by the edge of the sea . . . dwarfed by the immense thing that lay before it." Surf journalist **Ben Marcus** was equally unsparing, describing it as a "gray, sprawling wasteland" of decrepit buildings and oil derricks." Jan and Dean's sunny characterization has triumphed over the writers' caustic depictions,

at least in the popular imagination. The city has trademarked the phrase "Surf City USA" (Santa Cruz also laid claim to the title), which it can now use to promote events and hawk beachwear.

Huntington does have some legitimate claim to the title. Duke Kahanamoku, **the great Hawaiian surfer considered the father of modern surfing, gave surfing demonstrations here in the 1920s. In the 1960s (the Jan and Dean era), the United States Surfing Championships were held here;** Linda Benson **and** Joyce Hoffman **dueled for the women's titles, each winning four.** Huntington ceded the U.S. championship to other venues but was the site for the Op Pro in the 1980s and mid-'90s. **Frieda Zamba**, the Floridian who developed her technique in the erratic breaks off Daytona, took six championships at Huntington with a powerful, aggressive style that was then considered unfeminine (they had yet to witness the speed and power of **Lisa Andersen**,

Huntington Beach pier.

the Floridian juggernaut who slept under a bench and awakened, as from a fairy-tale dream, to consume every championship in sight).

Huntington is home of the annual Bank of the West Beach Games, which includes the U.S. Open of Surfing, a six-star World Qualifying Series event for the women's World Championship Tour. On a muggy July day at the 2006 Games, a carnival atmosphere prevailed, with beach volleyball, arcade games, Hawaiian shave ice and free bandanas from Target.

There were other sporting events that day—the British Open, in which Tiger Woods, still grieving over the death of his father, won with ruthless, almost uncanny precision; and the Tour de France, in which American cyclist Floyd Landis rode triumphantly down the Champs E'lysees to collect the yellow jersey.

While Woods and Landis accepted their trophies, young female surfers competed in the quarterfinals of the Junior Pro Division. One by one, these tiny forms, clad in a blue, red, yellow or white jersey, would crest upon the wave, desperately cutting and turning, trying to impress the judges in the stands with their style and strength and guts. The waves had height and punch, and there was the added problem that if you caught a left-breaking wave, you could end up smashed against the pilings of the pier.

In watching them battle it out, it was impossible not to reflect on those other athletic accomplishments—one on the roads and treacherous mountains of France; the other on the hardpack of the links at Royal Liverpool. But as unforgiving as were these environments, the roads did not suddenly shift or fall off; those bunkers and greens did not abruptly change their break in mid-shot.

These competitors were also up against another opponent: time. These heats did not go on forever; an impatient public wanted to see the men's longboarders, who were up next. So as the announcer ticked off the time through a megaphone—"Fifteen minutes, girls. . . . Eight minutes"—they knew they had to take what the ocean gave them and make the most of it. They would be bobbing out there, blue and red and yellow buoys, and suddenly one of them would launch herself upon a wave, and she would grab it and dig in, but the wave would simply give out, and she'd abort the run; she had to get back out and find another before the clock ran out. "Three minutes."

They were international, these girls. **Lee Ann Curren** was from Biaritتز, France. **Nikita Robb**, seventeen, from East London on the east coast of South Africa, surfed tough and lean but didn't make it to the next heat. Erica Hosseini, a highly regarded nine-teen-year-old from Newport Beach, won her heat. **Connie Arias**, nineteen, from Florida, lit up a wave with an 8.83 score, propelling her from fourth place to first in her heat. Afterwards, when asked about their performance, they seemed at a loss for words, like kids asked about their day at school. Something happened out there, but for whatever reason, they couldn't talk about it. Arias's board had an image of a curvaceous girl with wavy blonde hair. It was Paris Hilton, the heiress and media darling—"because she has done so much for society," Arias said, deadpan. Who says today's youth don't have a sense of irony?

In the finals, held the following week, no one could catch the girl in red—Lee Ann Curren, who perhaps had an edge on the other surfers, as she was the daughter of **Tom Curren**. A three-time world-champion surfer, Tom Curren had surfed brilliantly, with an original style, but his personal life followed an erratic path. He married a French teenager and made his home in Anglet, on the southwest coast of France, but he later divorced her and remarried, returning to take up residence in Santa Barbara. **But out of that Franco-American union came Lee Ann, and she inherited her father's surf-ing genes. At the Quiksilver ISA World Junior Surfing Championship in Brazil in May, she got into a tube in practice; standing upright, trailing her hand on the face, she acknowledged that "Dad taught me a bit about riding the tube." She went on to win the event.**

On that July day at Huntington, after Curren posted her third-consecutive Pro Junior victory, the announcer proclaimed that "a new legend begins," placing this heavy mantle upon her shoulders.

Layne Beachley inducted into the Surfing Walk of Fame in Huntington Beach, California, 2006.

When asked which surfer they most admired, all the juniors nodded and named one name: Sofia. They were referring to **Sofia Mulanovich**. Isn't that the Bulgarian gym-nast? Or maybe the pride of those surfing Latvians?

Actually, though of Serbo-Croatian lineage, Mulanovich is Peruvian, proudly so. Self-described as a "nor-mal girl who likes to surf," she grew up in Punta Hermosa, a small town

Sofia Mulanovich has taken the surfing world by storm. Photographer Jim Russi.

outside of Lima. One of the only girls to surf in Peru, she competed in the boys division, but she claims that "the boys loved that because it created a special bond between us."

WCT Rookie of the Year in 2003, Mulanovich became the first South American to win the World Championship Tour in 2004. "I've done this for my country and for all South Americans," said the Peruvian, nicknamed "La Gringa" for her blue eyes and sun-streaked hair. "Just to make a change and give them hope." ESPN awarded her with the 2005 ESPY for Best Female Sports Athlete; there is a monument to her outside the National Stadium in Lima.

Mulanovich took the title from Layne Beachley, owner of six world titles and one of women's surfing's most dominating figures. Beachley graciously conceded that "of all the girls on tour, I think Sofia's the most deserving of a world title."

Two days before, Beachley had been inducted into the Surfing Hall of Fame—"an enormous honor for a little Aussie battler," she said. "I marked my territory in Huntington Beach." Ironically, it was Beachley who had won the U.S. Open in 2005, amassing an overall score of 15.50, nearly two and a half more than her nearest competitor. "It's a matter of timing the sets," she said. "It was tough out there and you have to make the most of what there is to work with."

Perhaps Mulanovich recalled these words in 2006 as she went up against Australian **Jessi Miley-Dyer**. Hordes of people were swarming around the beach and pier, but most were watching beach volleyball or lining up for Hawaiian smoothies or simply pushing their way through the crowds—"controlled madness," in the words of Beachley, who was doing color commentary from the stands. "It can be overwhelming," the former Open champion told the crowd, "but also gratifying and rewarding." The stands were about half full as Mulanovich, who had started coming to the U.S. Open at age fourteen, and Miley-Dyer paddled out. The Peruvian wore red, the Aussie wore blue.

"La Gringa" goes for it! Photographer Jim Russi.

The waves, fed by a swell from a tropical storm over Baja, were three to five feet but unpredictable. Miley-Dyer grabbed a left-breaking wave but got caught in chop, the wave crumbling apart like a dry cracker. Then Mulanovich, showing "world-championship form" (Beachley), caught a right-hander that she worked like a pointillist painter, turning, cutting back, daubing away at this liquid palette before it finally gave out. Her 7.5 proved unbeatable; when the horn sounded, signaling the end of the contest, she was the new women's champion of the U.S. Open of Surfing.

"I'm really stoked," the twenty-three-year-old proclaimed at the awards ceremony, falling back on familiar surfer's argot. "It's been my dream to win the U.S. Open since I was very young, so it's amazing to finally do it."

Presented with a check for $4,500 and a brand-new Honda AquaTrax Jet Ski, Mulanovich thanked her boyfriend and her sponsors, which included Roxy and Red Bull. Then the two competitors, dripping wet, still in their jerseys, were herded off to the media tent, where they were not exactly mobbed by reporters. (Perhaps the journalists were conserving their energy for the men's event the next day.) Miley-Dyer, a cheerful twenty-year-old in her rookie season, admitted that being on tour and competing was "really hard." Even out of the water, the girls are all highly competitive; there is cheating at cards, tables overturned. "No worries," she said, satisfied, for the moment, with her second-place finish.

Mulanovich, shy, less confident in this venue than in the surf, would not own up to being a master strategist, outdueling her opponent by her patience and wave selection. She just grabbed a wave and went. In an interview with *Surf Life for Women*, she had confessed that "I have felt lonely many times because in a way I am different from everybody else on tour, different language and culture and sometimes beliefs." She is surfing, not just for herself, but all of Peru; she sees herself as "one of the only people lucky enough to follow my dreams." It is an opportunity that she cannot afford to let pass.

Now that she is in possession of her own Jet Ski, will she take on the big waves? She shakes her head, smiling. "I'm not that into it," she says. She has her work cut out for her, staving off the increasingly tough competitors on the women's tour and the charge from the young girls. "All the girls are ripping now," she says. This normal girl who loves to surf is now a championship-caliber surfer who travels the globe, ripping surf from Huntington to Brazil. Sometimes the loneliness, being separated from home and family, overwhelms her, but then it's back out in the water, another contest, another heat.

To follow the exploits of Sofia Mulanovich and those of the other young ripping female surfers, you must turn to the back pages of the sports section, when Tiger has won all the tournaments ten times over, when the drug scandal that threatened to strip Floyd Landis of his title finally dies down. There, you might catch a brief mention. Or perhaps you will see them out in the surf—blue, yellow, red, white—waiting for that one wave that will secure them a place in surfing history: world champion, Hall of Famer. But fame, that will remain as elusive as the perfect wave. *

CHAPTER 10

A Season IN THE SURF

Beachley, the "little Aussie battler." Photographer Jim Russi.

IT IS 2006, AND FROM FIJI TO FRANCE, BRAZIL TO MANLY BEACH TO THE SHORES OF HAWAI'I, THE BATTLE IS JOINED. THE BEST FEMALE SURFERS IN THE WORLD WILL MAKE THEIR PILGRIMAGE TO THESE SURF-ING HOLY GRAILS, AND THEY WILL TRY TO WREST FROM THE OCEAN AND FROM THEIR OWN HEARTS A VICTORY, and then another and another, and at the end one will be named the world champion of women's surfing. Will it be six-time world champion **Layne Beachley**, the "little Aussie battler"? Will it be one of the young upstarts—red-hot Peruvian **Sofia Mulanovich** or hard-charging **Chelsea Georgeson**, who pulled off a coup in 2005? Or will it be some unknown, some wild card who suddenly catches fire and begins outsurfing anything in the water?

Layne Beachley flashes the "stay loose" sign. Photographer Jim Russi.

The heir apparent to **Lisa Andersen**, Layne Beachley had the six world championships, but age and injuries had finally caught up with her, and an unprecedented seventh title seemed out of reach for this supremely talented surfer who was named number five in the world in the 2006 Surfer Poll.

But then, Layne Beachley's reach has always exceeded her grasp. Adopted as an infant, she lost her adoptive mother when she was six. Perhaps this double loss fueled her desire to surf, to find a home among the waves. At age four, she stole (borrowed) her brother's single-fin foam board, and while her dad sat on the sundeck of the Manly Surf Life-Saving Club, eating a sausage sandwich and drinking beer, she surfed.

Manly Beach was not a friendly environment. "I had to be one of the guys," recalled Beachley. "I had to surf as good as the guys, give as much shit as the guys and take as much as they could give me." And they gave and gave. They called her Gidget (apparently not realizing that it was the highest form of compliment). If she went north of the first storm-water pipe, she was told to go back to the southern end. She told them, "What are you, tomcats? You have to piss on your area, and I'm not allowed anywhere near it?" Layne discovered an age-old truth: the territorial male. But she wasn't having any of it—she went straight to the northern end.

She started competing professionally full time in 1991, struggling with the difficulties of life on tour: long plane rides; foreign languages, currencies and food; and being away from friends and family and the comforts of home for long periods of time. In 1993, she won the Diet Coke Women's Classic at Narrabeen, Australia, taking out no less than four-time world champion Lisa Andersen to reach the finals. **"I started believing in myself, which is what makes a huge difference, especially in competition,"** she said.

Chelsea takes it all in '05. Photographer Jim Russi.

Heading down to the surf.

In 1997, Beachley found herself making the finals of several events, finishing behind Andersen for the world title. "Somebody had to stop her!" said a determined Beachley. The following year, in France, Beachley scored an 8.5 and two 6.75s, which proved to be enough to win the world title. She hugged her then-boyfriend Ken Bradshaw and signed autographs. **"I knew this day would come," she said. "It was just a matter of time." Relieved that it was finally over, sometimes she would stop and think,** *F---, I did it!*

She did it five more times, sweeping aside the competition with her aggressive style to win her sixth world title in 2003. Then came a dry spell in which she was outmatched by the young upstarts—Sofia Mulanovich, the Peruvian wunderkind, unseated her as world champion in 2004.

The year 2005 marked the ascendancy of the new generation. Australian Chelsea Georgeson hit the trifecta, becoming the only one in the history of women's surfing to win the Billabong Pro Maui, the Vans Triple Crown of Surfing and the WCT title. "Winning the world championship was one of the best feelings I've ever had in my life," said the twenty-two-year-old goofyfooter. "It's something I've dreamed of and worked towards since I was a little girl growing up. You know, it's a huge sense of self-achievement. I train a lot, I train very hard for it, and it was just an overwhelming experience, you know. Being with my family and friends was just amazing."

Chelsea Georgeson is at one with this wave. Photographer Jim Russi.

Chelsea can rip!
Photographer Jim Russi.

It was Lisa Andersen who had seen Georgeson's championship potential and recruited her for the Roxy team. "Lisa Andersen used to come to Avalon where I used to surf every day," said Georgeson. "I thought that was amazing. I had never seen a woman surfer before. Seeing a four-time world champion surfing at my own break was so inspiring, and she surfed so much like a guy. She was so good and her style was insane."

Georgeson also paid obeisance to Layne Beachley. "Layne is a huge inspiration for women surfers. Six world titles is an amazing accomplishment. I don't know how she did it."

If you parse that sentence—particularly the use of the past tense ("don't know how she did it")—you get the sense that Beachley has had her quotient of championships, and now the time has come for the new generation to claim its due portion.

But 2006 was a new season, and Beachley was ready to reclaim her title. The year did not start out as Beachley hoped—but it was not the young whippersnappers at her heels, it was thirty-one-year-old Australian Melanie Redman-Carr. She hadn't won since the Roxy Pro in Fiji in 2002, but she started out the 2006 season on fire, winning three events in a row, including a close win over Beachley at the Roxy Pro on Australia's Gold Coast. It was déjà vu all over again for Beachley, whom Redman-Carr had beaten in 2002 in a WQS event on this same break.

Redman-Carr sensed blood in the water. "I would have liked to beat her by more," she said. The two Australians—the "golden girls"—met again in the Roxy Pro Fiji, in six- to eight-feet conditions that favored both surfers. Beachley's aggressive style was not enough to outduel the methodical Redman-Carr. Then, at Teahupoo in Tahiti, notorious for its molecule-altering barrels, there was another showdown. **Chelsea Georgeson, who scored the only 10 of the day, said of the sudden resurgence in 2006 of her older counterparts: "It's pretty crazy. They probably saw the headlines in Australia—'Two Old Birds Have Their Day,' or something—and it fired them up." It was Redman-Carr who had her day. Aglow from her trifecta, she said, "Everything is transpiring in my favor."**

Ah, hubris.

Chelsea Georgeson.
Photographer Jim Russi.

In August, at the Billabong Girls Pro in Brazil, Redman-Carr did not even make it out of the first heat. Beachley, meanwhile, advanced to the finals against fellow Australian **Jessi Miley-Dyer**, a rookie on the WCT tour and a finalist at the U.S. Surfing Open in Huntington Beach. Displaying the aggressive form that had made her the reigning queen of women's surfing for six years, Beachley posted scores of 9.95 and 8.5. **"The insatiable winning thirst has come back," she said.**

Now it was off to France for the Rip Curl Pro Mademoiselle at Les Bourdaines. French surf, like escargot and truffles, is an acquired taste, and Redman-Carr found she didn't have much of an appetite. **"I was drifting around out there, hoping it would end," she said, hardly the ringing words of a confident soon-to-be-champion. She finished second to Chelsea Georgeson, who had recovered her 2005 winning form. "I'm just happy to have my first win this year," said a relieved Georgeson, adding in an outburst of Francophile fervor,**

"France has always been a really special place for me. I love coming here. I love the people and the place."

In October, Beachley would take on all comers on her home break at Manly Beach. Redman-Carr drifted out of the contest in the early heat, leaving it wide open for Beachley. In the semifinals, she polished off Georgeson, who admitted, "It just wasn't my day." Beachley waited for Sofia Mulanovich to win her semi, but time ran out for the Peruvian, who was riding a replacement because her board broke earlier. The winner was a wild-card entry, nineteen-year-old Australian **Stephanie Gilmore, who had surprised a lot of people in 2005 when she became the youngest-ever winner of an ASP World Tour event.**

Against Beachley in the finals, the Gilmore girl told herself, "Go, get a wave, girl, go!" and blasted away on a right-hander for a 7. Beachley, meanwhile, was desperately trying to find a decent ride in this wave-starved heat. She went to her "little secret spot," but the clock kept ticking down. . . 23. . . 13. . . 7 . . . tick . . . tick . . . tick . . . and the horn sounded. It was Stephanie Gilmore who emerged from the surf with the victory. "I guess they were thinking, 'Oh, wild card. We can just cruise a bit,'" said Gilmore, whose upset of Beachley put her firmly in the ranks of the world's elite surfers.

Chelsea Georgeson (top) and Sofia Mulanovich (bottom). Photographer Jim Russi.

Afterwards, a disappointed Beachley, who had organized the event, said, "Aren't I foolish? Why did I invite Stephanie Gilmore?" In answer to her half-joking rhetorical question, it was to ensure a high level of surfing—and she managed to hold on to her number-one ranking, thanks to Redman-Carr's defeat.

Sofia Mulanovich, the pride of Peru. Photographer Jim Russi.

Next it was off to the North Shore of Oahu, the ancient proving ground for surfers, for the Vans Triple Crown. Beachley could clinch at the Roxy Pro at Sunset . . . but the surf gods are capricious, especially in Hawai'i.

"KUMAI!" ("ARISE!")

The cry arose from the crowd at Haleiwa's Ali'i Beach Park, site of the Op Pro Hawai'i, the first contest in the Vans Triple Crown.

"Kumai!" This time louder, more urgently.

The surf had lain flat for days, mocking the efforts of these humans and their surfing contest. On the morning of November 15, a powerful 8.1 earthquake rattled the tectonic plates off the coast of Japan, and a tidal wave warning was posted for the Hawaiian Islands. The tides rose a few feet, boats were temporarily dry-docked, debris washed up on the shore. But for that surge, the surf remained stubbornly flat.

The contest could not be held any longer—and so at 12:30 p.m., the contestants and onlookers gathered for the ancient Hawaiian blessing. The contestants were anointed with water dispensed with a palm frond, and then the congregants were led in a desperate entreaty for waves: "Kumai!"

Despite some dazzling performances by emerging young talent, all the usual suspects made it out of their heats to the semifinals: Beachley, Mulanovich, Redman-Carr—and that Gilmore girl again! "Happy Gilmore," they were calling her, and well she should have been—her smooth, stylish performance on erratic waves carrying her into the finals.

Redman-Carr, desperately struggling for waves, was called for an interference, which seemed to wipe out any momentum she may have had; Beachley couldn't find traction on the mostly left-breaking sets. That left three South Americans—Mulanovich and two Brazilians, Jacqueline Silva and Taís Almeida—to face Gilmore in the championship round.

All the contestants came in, everyone, that is, but Beachley. She stayed out, grappling with the surf, determined to catch a decent wave. **The announcer attempted to coax her in, calling out through the bullhorn, "Here comes a good wave, Layne. Grab that one." But she was on Layne time and ignored this voice from the shore; finally, reluctantly, she relinquished the surf to the finalists. "I had Haleiwa all to myself," she said.**

Mulanovich wasted no time, booming out on a left-breaking wave for an 8.17. Her two-wave total of 15.84 proved insurmountable. "I really worked for it," she said. "I hustled out there." The difference was that she was comfortable on her backhand, and Gilmore, who came in second, was not. All four finalists were presented with handmade leis and a Hawaiian carving; Mulanovich also pocketed $4,500. "I love surfing Haleiwa," she said. "Hawai'i's the place to win!" No doubt she was already imagining further Hawaiian triumphs at the Roxy Pro, down the road at Sunset.

Beachley, meanwhile, was relaxed and confident, "just having fun." She had learned not to cross that fine line where she expects too much. "I have no bigger critic than me," she says, adding, "I have nothing left to prove." True, but in this comeback season, one can sense that she is salivating to get to Sunset and really strut her stuff: "They call me Mrs. Sunset," she reminds us.

WILL THE SUN SET ON MRS. SUNSET?

Mrs. Sunset did not make it out of the semifinals in the Roxy Pro, the penultimate event in the Vans Triple Crown. It was another pesky wild card. Melanie Bartels, from the west side of Oahu, wasn't even supposed to be in the competition, but at the last minute Silvana Lima dropped out because of injury, and Bartels found herself in the finals against fellow wild card entry Stephanie Gilmore. "Mel and I were paddling out, and we gave ourselves a little high-five," Gilmore said. "We went, 'Wow, it's pretty cool we both made it all the way from the trials, so let's take it to the top, and that's what we did."

Layne Beachley displays the form that won her seven world titles. Photographer Jim Russi.

Except that Bartels did it just a bit more—she caught a wave with fourteen seconds left to edge out that Gilmore girl.

What made the difference? "I think something has clicked because even in the trials there were heats where I wanted to give up," Bartels said. "But as soon as that negativity came into my head, I went 'Think positive,' and that made me think that I still had a chance, and I stuck to my game plan and turned that negative into a positive. It worked in every heat, and I came out winning."

The season was on the wane—one more leg of the Triple Crown, one more grueling competition with all those heats. Out of the surf at Honolua Bay, a champion would emerge. In this streaky season of wild cards and improbable dark horses, even the handicappers in Vegas (not that they actually handicap women's surf contests) couldn't pick this one.

And what a setting for the final showdown. Four-time world champion Mark Richards called Honolua Bay "the best wave in the world." This right-breaking wave on Maui's northwest shore was the staging area for the shortboard revolution in the 1970s; its allure has not diminished over the years, thanks to its ability to form into deliciously long, fast-moving barrels. The conditions for Billabong Pro were nearly perfect—four- to six-foot sets that provided amped-up, battle-worthy waves.

Keala Kennelly—a no-holds-barred barrel rider affectionately known as KK—was a beneficiary. In the final heat, she caught a bomb and tucked into the tube. **"I was within inches away from a 10 and claiming the whole thing," said KK.**

Jessi Miley-Dyer, who had caught the next wave, said, "My heart just dropped down to the floor thinking; she just beat me in the last second of the heat." Then KK stood up to start her victory dance—and she got clipped in the head. "I started celebrating too early, but it's cool," she said philosophically. **And so it was Miley-Dyer who took the Billabong as well as Rookie of the Year honors.**

Though she came in third at the Billabong, Sofia Mulanovich amassed enough total points to earn the Vans Triple Crown title. "It has been a year of experience for me," the Peruvian remarked. "I feel that I have grown a lot as a surfer and a person. Triple Crown was the icing on the cake." Indeed—she pocketed a cool ten grand. "I'm stoked—ten thousand bucks!"

And what of Layne Beachley? "Leading into this I was a little bit nervous," she admitted. "Sunset was a good lesson for me because I had opportunity there and I blew it. Now I realize that it just comes down to me and the ocean and just being in tune with Mother Nature."

She and Mother Nature were at one on the first day of competition. "When I pulled into that barrel in the first wave of that heat, I was just inside this massive cavern, thinking, I'm coming out of it," she said. "There was no apprehension, no anxiety, no nerves, just full confidence and love of surfing Honolua Bay."

This buoyant attitude carried her into the semifinals, where she lost to Miley-Dyer. But no matter—with Georgeson having been eliminated in the quarterfinals, the WCT championship was hers. It was an amazing comeback, a year of mastering self-doubt and measuring herself against the covetousness and audaciousness of youth.

Did this mean she would go for an eighth world title—an exalted stature enjoyed only by that most high in the pantheon of surfing gods, Kelly Slater? "It means I'm going for eight and Kelly better not win nine!" joked the little Aussie battler. "It means I'm going to go out there and have some more fun. I think Kelly is going to go for ten, and if he does, he can have it!"

Oh, but she shall have it, too, for unless the oceans roll back and become as ponds and the swells vanish into oblivion and the surfboards crumble unto dust, she will be out there, claiming her portion. Soph and Chels and KK and Jess, they will have their day, their year—but not just yet. *

Hawaiians Unleashed

Where have all the Hawaiians gone? Has the legacy of two of the greatest female surfers of all time, Rell Sunn and Margo Oberg, become the flotsam of history? Have the keepers of the aloha spirit been swept under by the Australian juggernaut, overpowered by the South American onslaught? The women's surf scene today is a crowded polyglot of styles and accents and surf breaks; perhaps Hawai'i has seen its day in the sun.

Rest easy, Rell. Margo, take heart. Your legacies are in the best possible hands (and feet and hearts). The ancient sport of surfing, which had all but vanished from the islands in the 1890s, is enjoying a Hawaiian renaissance. There is Roche and Keala and Megan and Melanie, and coming up fast behind them, Carissa and Coco and Malia.

Layne Beachley once remarked of Rochelle Ballard, "When it comes to barrel riding, she's the Kelly Slater of women's surfing." This is high praise indeed; Slater, who captured a record eighth WCT championship in 2006, is the consummate tube rider, with a signature no-hands stance that won him five Pipeline Masters titles. Ballard pays homage to Oberg, a fellow Kawaian, for helping to develop her tube-riding skills. "It was pretty cool, just hanging out with her and learning how to ride big waves," Ballard recalls.

To be compared to Slater elevates Ballard into the pantheon of surfing gods. In the mid-'90s it was rare to see a woman riding the tube, but Ballard took on such legendary tubes as Backdoor Pipe and Teahupoo, touching off an explosion of female tube riding—and grudging admiration from the men. "I love it when guys go, 'Oh my gosh, did you see what that woman just did?'" she said in an interview with *Surfer* magazine's Justin Cote.

In 1997, her first year on the WCT, she finished sixth overall. Pro surfer John Shimooka, writing in *H3O* magazine, took exception to the numbers: "She surfs unreal and charges whether it's two feet or ten feet. She always goes for it, so her rating to me is just a number." His faith in her proved justified: in 1999, Ballard made surfing history by scoring two perfect 10s riding tubes at Burleigh, Australia. "You're in the barrel and there's this quiet rumble," Ballard said, "there's so much energy in that rumble, the sound of the ocean's power."

The year 2002 was a breakout year for Ballard—she won *Surfer* magazine's annual Surfer Poll, and she was the stunt double for the 2002 film *Blue Crush*—that final scene, a perfect ten in the tube, provided a dramatic, highly cinematic ending to a film that helped to legitimize women's surfing.

Keala Kennelly, Ballard's good friend and competitor, shares her passion for barrel riding. Born in Hanalei, Kauai, and raised in a geodesic dome that was built by her surfer parents, she took surfing to a new level with her aerial acrobatics and fearless tube riding that led *Rolling Stone* magazine to anoint her as Hawai'i's big-wave Amazon. **In an epic tube ride, she scored a perfect 10 at the Billabong Pro in Tahiti in 2001.**

For Megan Abubo, **the ocean is a way of life.** She was born in Connecticut but moved to Haleiwa on the North Shore in time to rescue her from a life of preppie triviality. She developed into one of the world's most accomplished female surfers, a twelve-year veteran of the tour who finished second to Layne Beachley in the 2000 WCT rankings and battled Chelsea Georgeson and Sophia Mulanovich for the 2005 title. She has a passion for tow-in surfing—she likes it out on the outer reefs where it's just you and the ocean. A stunt double in *Blue Crush*, she also did a provocative layout for *Rolling Stone* in which she posed in the nude with a surfboard in front as a modesty panel.

Abubo joined with Ballard and others in founding the International Women's Surfing, a lobbying group that helped to raise the minimum mandatory prize money for WCT events from $30,000 to $60,000. Seeking out and developing young talent is also a personal mission for Ballard. The annual Rochelle Ballard O'Neill Surf Camp, held on her home island of Kauai, teaches technique and competitive strategy, with an evening skate session and hip-hop lesson. The camp has groomed Hawai'i's most promising young surfers, including Coco Ho and Malia Manuel.

"I saw the potential in these girls, and their surfing has come such a long way," says Ballard. "I think in another five years' time, Hawai'i will dominate the WCT. I'm glad to contribute to the growth of women's surfing in Hawai'i, and I'm grateful that my sponsors O'Neill and Reef recognize the importance and share my passion for supporting the up-and-coming youth."

To give these aspiring surfers a taste of pro competition, the second-annual O'Neill Island Girl Junior Pro, supported by Reef and Nukumoi Surf Co., was held at Poipu in 2006. The winner earned a slot in round one of the Op Pro Hawai'i, the six-star WQS event that is the first jewel of the Vans Triple Crown of Surfing. **Malia Manuel, a twenty-year-old from Kauai surfing in her first professional contest, was the high scorer with perfectly executed turns and flashy 360s. "I felt confident after I got a couple, so I thought I'd go for it," said Manuel.**

At the OP Pro Hawai'i at Haleiwa, Manuel again proved she could hold her own against the best in the world, advancing out of her trial heats. But the talk of the tournament was **Carissa Moore** of Oahu. The youngest to surf this event, the fourteen-year-old high school freshman electrified the crowd with scores of 8.17 and 7.1. When asked for an interview, she said, "I'll have to ask my dad." It was he who taught her to surf in Waikiki, and she has emerged from that

Megan Abubo has an abundance of talent.

tutelage with a riskier, more aggressive style of surfing—the "new school" of women's surfing. Moore is wisely biding her time, planning to finish school, waiting for her moment in the sun. **"I'll try my best and see what happens," she says.**

Carissa Moore has an insider's knowledge of Hawaiian surf.
Photographer Jim Russi.

Her best proved more than enough at the 2007 NSAA National Championships at Lower Trestles in California—the Super Bowl of youth surfing. As the clock ticked down to the final minute in the Women's Final, Moore caught a right-hander and dazzled the crowd with skillful cutbacks and a mini-air to earn a 9.75 out of 10. "I just went out in the Open final and just tried to have fun and forget about the pressure," said the Hawaiian goofyfooter.

Melanie Bartels has also drunk from the sweet cup of victory. Growing up on Oahu's west side, Bartels took the bus to surf at Makaha, and it was "Auntie Rell" (Rell Sunn) who encouraged her, taking her and a group of young Hawaiian surfers to France. "She had a lot of aloha, a lot of heart," Bartels says.

Four friends surfing at Waikiki.

Not known as a strong finisher at contests, Bartels took everyone by surprise at the Roxy Pro Hawai'i in 2006 by upsetting Georgeson, Beachley, and the rest, for her first-ever WCT win. "For the first time I really believed in myself, believed in my surfing," Bartels said. "I went, 'this might be my time, you know, because everyone has their time.' It was definitely my time today—hopefully it will still be my time next year."

It is her time, the time for the Hawaiians. She led a Hawaiian-laden Team USA into the treacherous surf at Puerto Escondido, Mexico—the "Mexican Pipeline"—for the 2007 X Games. Up against a world team stacked with talent—Stephanie Gilmore, Sofia Mulanovich et al.—the Americans seemed outmatched. But Ballard took off and got inside a tube, scoring a 7.0. Then Bartels worked her way into a long right-hand barrel, earning an 8.5. "I didn't think I was going to make it out," said Bartels. "It was my longest barrel ever." The match went down to the wire, but thanks to Bartels and her cheering squad, the U.S. came out on top, 55–52. "What a complete rush!" exclaimed U.S. coach Lisa Andersen, savoring the American triumph over the world squad, led by arch-rival Layne Beachley. "I haven't felt this feeling since I won a contest back in 2001."

Mahalo to these young women, the heirs to the legacy of Rell and Margo; with their talent and generosity, they will provide a continuum between past and future, honoring that almost holy alliance between Hawaiians and the surf. *

The LONG

Above: Renowned longboarder Kassia Meador shows her free-surfing form.
Opposite: Don't sell shortboarders short!

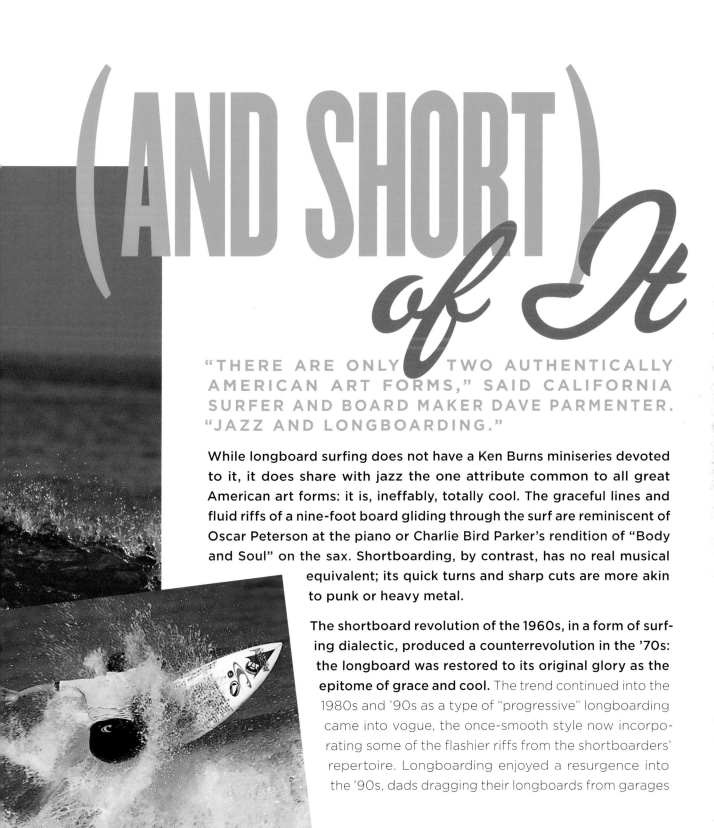

CHAPTER 11

(AND SHORT) of It

"THERE ARE ONLY TWO AUTHENTICALLY AMERICAN ART FORMS," SAID CALIFORNIA SURFER AND BOARD MAKER DAVE PARMENTER. "JAZZ AND LONGBOARDING."

While longboard surfing does not have a Ken Burns miniseries devoted to it, it does share with jazz the one attribute common to all great American art forms: it is, ineffably, totally cool. The graceful lines and fluid riffs of a nine-foot board gliding through the surf are reminiscent of Oscar Peterson at the piano or Charlie Bird Parker's rendition of "Body and Soul" on the sax. Shortboarding, by contrast, has no real musical equivalent; its quick turns and sharp cuts are more akin to punk or heavy metal.

The shortboard revolution of the 1960s, in a form of surfing dialectic, produced a counterrevolution in the '70s: the longboard was restored to its original glory as the epitome of grace and cool. The trend continued into the 1980s and '90s as a type of "progressive" longboarding came into vogue, the once-smooth style now incorporating some of the flashier riffs from the shortboarders' repertoire. Longboarding enjoyed a resurgence into the '90s, dads dragging their longboards from garages

121

and putting their kids on them. Surf shops specializing in longboards opened up and down the California coast, and more than one hundred longboard clubs sprang up around the world. It was a form of nostalgia, evoking that innocent time of woodies and bushy-bushy blond hairdos—only this time, the girls didn't have to stand on the shore and watch as the guys surfed; they were out there as well, walking the nose, reinventing the surfing mythology with themselves in it.

Competitively, it took some time for the longboard to work its way back into the surf lineup: in 1986, a longboard division was added to the men's world pro tour. It wasn't until 1999 that the women finally had their own longboard division on the pro tour. In the three-day event held at Boca Barranca, Costa Rica, fifty-two women competed for a total purse of $4,000. The winner was **Daize Shayne**, a goofyfooter from Hawai'i who became the poster girl for women's surfing. Runner-up **Cori Schumacher** from California won the following year despite having a mild concussion and stitches in her leg from rolling her car on the freeway the week before. **Kim Hamrock**, a.k.a. Danger Woman, won in 2002.

In 2005, three generations of women came from all over the world to compete in the three divisions of the tournament, which was held at Ocean Beach, California. Five-time U.S. champion Linda Benson had taken over the running of the tournament from founder Hank Raymond. "Linda is a legend," Raymond said. "She is the face of women's longboard surfing. I couldn't imagine anyone else taking this to the future."

Determined to pull it off, despite the lack of financial support, Benson scrounged for money to put toward the purse, securing $12,500 from sponsors and $2,000 from Hansen's Surfboards, a local surfshop.

For the first two days, the tournament had been more of a ballet performance, the women dancing a dainty pas de deux with the waves, but on that final Sunday, "the ocean had turned macho," as described by *San Diego Union-Tribune* writer Terry Rodgers—the scene of high drama, people screaming on the beach, the waves growing bigger and more ferocious by the hours. "It was like Woodstock," Benson said. Kristy Murphy, a twenty-eight-year-old goofyfooter from Florida, rode the wild California surf to a world title. Midway through the heat, she caught an overhead left and strutted her

Surfing off the Central California coast.

Alana Mock, NSAA Contest,
Girls Semi-Finals, Kona, Hawai'i.

stuff, walking the nose and hanging five. Her bravura performance earned her an 8.17, the highest
score for a single wave in the finals.

The men offered grudging, if condescending, admiration for the women's performance. "These
ladies surfed waves that were almost unsurfable," said local legend Jim "Mouse" Robb. Skip Frye,
who had surfed in tournaments back in the '60s and '70s, said, "After what I saw today, I only
have this to say: 'Women rock!'"

**Women and their longboards, no longer just a pretty face on the surf scene, had proven that
they could take on an ocean juiced with testosterone and give back everything they got and
then some. The ASP, that surf-organization-come-lately, finally decided to hold the first-ever
ASP-sanctioned world championship, this one in Biarritz, France.**

**How is it that longboarding—one of only two authentic American art forms—came to be held
in France?** There is a curious Gallic appetite for that which Americans have relegated to the
Smithsonian closet or discarded altogether. Just as jazz found its way into the smoky clubs of

Paris, just as Jerry Lewis (somewhat inexplicably) was embraced as a comic genius, so, too, did surfing find a toehold on French soil.

Lee Ann Curren, daughter of surfing legend **Tom Curren**, grew up in France and offered this assessment: "France is cold." Her comment refers not to the sometimes chilly French hauteur, but to actual climatic conditions. "Sometimes you surf when it's snowing," she said.

That is in winter; in summer, sunnier conditions prevail. Twenty miles north of the Spanish border is the seaside resort of Biarritz, European headquarters for Quiksilver, the surfwear giant. Biarritz, which since 1992 had hosted the annual Biarritz Surf Festival, had its eye on the prize when it courted the women's pro tour: the tourist dollar. With Evian as a sponsor, and a soupçon of French glamor to smarten up the sometimes déclassé surf scene, the stage was elegantly set for the first-annual Roxy Women's World Longboard Championship.

Surfing in clean three-footers (hardly the white knucklers of the year before in Ocean Beach), sixty women competed for a total purse of $30,000 and the right to be called the first ASP-sanctioned world champion. The entire heat was dominated by nineteen-year-old Californian Schuyler McFerran. **Surfing against veterans whom she had looked up to when she was starting out in longboarding, she posted a 9.25 for her skillful nose riding.** Afterwards, she noted, "Some people were really stoked for me, and some people seemed kind of bummed." McFerran may have been bummed by the prize money—a mere $4,500—but she had earned a place in the record books as the Women's World Longboard champion.

With longboarding having taken its place on the international stage, it appeared that California, once the proud epicenter of the surf scene, had apparently been relegated to the backwater of surfing.

A sweet riff . . .

Followed by a kiss!

Except that **Linda Benson** wasn't having any of it. She wasn't about to let longboarding vanish into the California fog, consigned to a dim and distant nostalgia. While recognizing that having two contests lay claim to the world championship was not in the best interests of women's surfing, she wasn't about to concede this sport, this art form that she had pioneered forty years ago and still loved, to any French group, no matter how impressive its wine list or elegant its couture.

Linda Benson is diminutive in size, quiet in demeanor, but there's something about her that's difficult to say no to. She contacted Roxy and began, in the same relentless way in which she tracked down six U.S. championships, to campaign for the surfwear maker to sponsor an event in California. At Benson's steady insistence, Roxy finally agreed to foot the money for an ASP-sanctioned U.S. longboard championship at Cardiff Reef, a beach town south of Oceanside, in September 2006.

Would the ocean, which had been lazing around like a cat in the sun all summer, rouse itself up in time for the event? "If the gods are with us," Benson said. The gods, though capricious, could not deny this legend of surfing: the waves, while not the testosterone monsters of the year before, put the eighty competitors to the test. The arcane judging criteria called for **"Radical Controlled Maneuvers in the Critical Section of a Wave with Speed, Form and Flow to Maximize Scoring Potential."** No doubt these words were a source of inspiration for the surfers struggling to survive the early heats and make it to the finals.

The mood on Saturday was relaxed and convivial as the surfers paddled out in the early heats, a long, languid day of sun and waves. The next day, the waves were not macho, but they had plenty of heft and speed; you could look very, very good or very, very bad. In the semifinals, Jennifer Smith caught a wave and danced on the nose like an angel on the head of a

Great waves, cold water . . .

Should we go out?

Yeah, go for it!

Linda Benson, a living surf legend, showed them how it's done at the 2006 Roxy Jam at Cardiff Reef, California.

pin, posting the day's highest score: a near-perfect 9.8. But conditions deteriorated in the finals, and it was Lindsay Steinriede, surfing a steady, quiet heat, who posted dual 6.75s, modest but adequate to take the championship. Two-time champion Cori Schumacher, who came in second, was decidedly not stoked at the results: "Nothing really manifested for the rest of us," she said, referring to the vagaries of the waves. Smith lamented that she may have peaked a bit too early in the semifinals. The strategy that had served her well that morning, holding position and waiting for the best wave, failed her in the afternoon, when the waves were not as predictable or generous, while Steinriede took what nature gave her and emerged triumphant.

Brittany surf team at Cote des Basques, Biarritz.

Lindsay Steinriede (left) wins the Linda Benson Women's Longboard Pro, Cardiff Reef, 2006.

When asked why she surfed longboards rather than shortboards, the new women's champion paused, her board under her arm, as though considering this question for the first time. Was she pondering the legacy of longboarders, the graceful elegance of a longboard on a wave, her place in this most American of art forms? Finally she said, "It's easier to catch waves." There it is. Not the beauty or the history or the art; it's a means to an end: catching waves. There was no time to savor her victory; it was home to study for a kinesiology test at eight the next morning.

Steinriede and the other competitors demonstrated, yet again, the skill and accomplishment of female longboarders, handling themselves with great confidence and grace in the surf. But what stole that day—indeed, the entire tournament—were the legends who surfed a heat

Left: This longboard looks good in stripes.
Right: Legendary longboarder Jericho Poppler at the 2006 Roxy Jam.

before the finals. **Linda Benson**, **Jericho Poppler**, the great **Lisa Andersen**—they tumbled into the water like Chinese acrobats, surfing singly or in tandem, the women doing handstands on the men's shoulders. "Jericho's a real wave hog," the announcer joked. In her bright red one-piece suit, riding a banana-yellow longboard, Poppler was like a bright flash of tropical wing against the blue surf. *Look,* she and the others seemed to say, *here is how it's done.* You could feel their burning hunger

Julie Cox, Margaritaville Longboard Open, 2002, Steamer's Lane, Santa Cruz, California.

Heading home after a long day of longboarding.

for waves, their delighting in their moment in the sun. When the horn sounded the end of the heat, they reluctantly ceded the waves to their progeny, the young women longboarders who make it look so easy because there had been Benson and Poppler and Andersen. **Without them, there would be no contest, no cheering crowds, and they would be standing on the shore watching the guys.** ✳

Two young surfers with their fish boards.

Inspiration: Angela Madsen

Angela Madsen is a paraplegic—"differently abled," is how she would put it. An ex-Marine and competitive rower, Madsen suffered spinal cord damage following surgery to repair an injury sustained while in the service. An indomitable figure who is planning to row across the Atlantic with a fellow paraplegic, she surfs competitively at longboard contests around the world and was the talk of the beach at the 2006 Roxy Pro. In August, she packed up her Pope ten-foot bisect board and headed to Biarritz, France, for the World Longboard Championships, not knowing if she would be allowed to participate. She was allowed in the contest, but the airlines had misplaced an important piece of luggage—her surfboard. Using a borrowed ten-foot yellow slab of a board that she would select for the Huntington Beach Longboard Crew Surfing Club Pier Paddle Race on New Year's Day "but probably for nothing else," she competed against the best female longboarders in the world. **Following is an excerpt from the diary she kept while attending that contest.**

Angela Madsen surfing at the Huntington Longboard Crew Paddle.

CONTEST DAY 5– FRIDAY, JULY 7: I took a cab today because I thought screaming down the hills at thirty miles per hour in the wheelchair with the surfboard may be too dangerous. Small and clean again. Finally an opportunity to surf my board. I went out for a bit before the quarterfinals began. There was a concert at a beach amphitheater not far from the contest site we all went to this evening. Our group was sitting in the middle of the sandy beach just behind Linda Benson and some of the parents. Linda looked back at me and made mention that my being there at "Biarritz, France, traveling alone" took guts, and she shook my hand.

CONTEST DAY 6– SATURDAY, JULY 8—THE SEMI AND FINALS: The waves were slightly bigger and continued to increase in size throughout the day. I do not think it got bigger than 1.5 meters though. Still clean with some pretty fun waves. The tides and surf change so radically there, but Schuyler McFerran surfed the most consistently throughout. Between the semi-finals and the finals they had an expression session. About twenty-five people signed up to surf in it. It was crowded. With the tide the conditions were not very good. I decided not to participate. After the final the tide was changing, it was not crowded and it was looking like a lot of fun, so I went out then.

I was surfing the best I had surfed in a long time in chest- to head-high sets. Wave after wave. I had a beautiful ride that I took nearly all the way in to the rocks to discover that most everyone in surfer's

village was watching me. I was riding waves, doing switch stance, floaters and re-entry, cutbacks, even a hang five. They were all cheering and carrying on. I had my own personal expression session and did one of the things I had set out to do. **Disability awareness and education, changing the perception of what people think or know differently abled people can do!** The other surfers from the contest began popping up in the lineup, and then I had done one of the other things I had set out to do. I had surfed with some of the best women longboarders on the planet. **I had accomplished and done everything I had set out to do.** *

A young surfer tests the waters of Cote des Basques, Biarritz, France.

The Surf Breaks of the
APOCALYPSE

PIPELINE. JAWS. MAVERICK'S.

THEY CARRY, IN THEIR MOUNTAINOUS SWELLS, THE WILD-NESS OF THE OCEAN, THE ENERGY OF NATURE RAW AND UNLEASHED. THEY ROLL ACROSS THE OCEAN UNIMPEDED, AND GOD HELP ANYONE WHO HAS THE HUBRIS OR SHEER INSANITY TO GET IN THEIR WAY. THEY SNAP SURFBOARDS IN TWO. THEY FLING SURFERS INTO THE TUMULT OF WATER AND HOLD THEM DOWN ONCE, TWICE, THREE TIMES. DARE TO RIDE ME, WILL YOU?

Yet there are some surfers who simply cannot resist risking life and limb for the sake of the ultimate ride on the world's biggest, baddest waves. Even women (even, because as a rule women are a sensible lot and do not succumb to these testosterone-driven challenges) have braved the big waves.

Why would anyone, male or female, risk injury and even death to ride these waves? Is it a kind of madness, a death wish?

Shane Murphy, a sports psychologist and professor at Western Connecticut State University who has worked with Olympians and other athletes, argues that the perspective of extreme athletes is very different from our own. "We look at a risky situation and know that if we were in that situation we would be out of control, " he said. "But from the athletes' perspective, they have a lot of control, and there are a lot of things that they do to minimize risk."

These athletes redefine risk using a combination of skills, experience and environment. "I've worked with groups climbing Everest, including one group without oxygen," Murphy said. "To me that just seems like the height of risk. But [the climbers] took every precaution they could think of. To them it was the next step in an activity that they've done for years. They weren't going out there to get hurt."

In the calculus of risk-reward, the payoff of an extreme sport such as big-wave surfing is measured in adrenaline rush versus the danger posed by the conditions. In January 1998 at Outer Logs, the surf break between Pipeline and Waimea, the waves were so massive that only a dozen surfers risked going out. Ken Bradshaw, **who caught a wave estimated to be between forty and forty-five feet, said, "You come face to face with yourself. What sort of fear you can handle."**

Layne Beachley, then six-time world champion and Ken Bradshaw's girlfriend, was on the shore watching—"we knew our limits," she said of those who did not go out. But she wanted to test herself on this break. With Bradshaw as her tow-in partner, she caught a twenty-five-foot wave. "I know I didn't go deep enough . . . but I did a little turn and a fade, I actually surfed the wave. **I remember kicking out and just screaming, 'Yeah!' It was such an amazing feeling, so adrenalizing. I got back to the machine and went, 'That's it, I'm hooked. I'm a junkie.'"**

Kassia Meador, a California surfer, experienced that blood-pounding combination of terror and exhilaration at Sunset. "My first time out at Sunset was the day of truth," she recalled in *Honolulu* magazine. "One wave in particular I was paddling like crazy. I finally got locked into it and it was like, 'Okay, it is too late to back down.' The drop seemed like it was never going to end, and my heart beat faster than ever before. I was high off the adrenaline for the rest of the day."

The prospect of this adrenaline high seems to outweigh the obvious risks. All big-wave surfers, male and female, have experienced injury and terrifying hold-downs, where you wipe out and struggle to the surface, only to be pushed down by the next wave. Honolulu lifeguard captain James Howe points out, "The ocean doesn't discriminate. It doesn't care who you are, what you are or how strong you are. The ocean is bigger, and it can grab you at any time." He recalled the time that "North Shore Sally," who was surfing at Haleiwa on the North Shore, got caught in a section known as the Toilet Bowl, which is only a few inches deep at the edge of the wave. She wiped out and got slammed face-first on the bottom. She survived but ended up disfigured. During the filming of *AKA: Girl Surfer,* one of the surfers got knocked out underwater and had to be medevaced to the hospital. "It was fortunate she survived," Howe said.

Think girls don't have what it takes to surf the big waves?
Think again! Emilia Perry on Oahu's North Shore.

Once an exclusively male domain, the big waves are now equally, obsessively, sought after by female big-wave surfers; indeed, it is almost de rigueur that you take on the big waves if you want to maintain your surf cred.

PIPELINE

Pipeline is the Hollywood bad boy of surf breaks: brooding, intense, unpredictable, but capable of flashes of brilliance. Located on Oahu's North Shore, west of Waimea Bay, Pipe has become among the sexiest, most glamorous of the big waves. Pipeline's First Reef forms one of surfing's best tubes. Second Reef and Third Reef are located farther offshore, and there is Backdoor, a right-breaking wave that materializes during a north or northwest swell. Surfers love Pipe not only for the challenge it poses but for the gallery of photographers on the shore, recording their exploits. The Chantays' hit instrumental "Pipeline" helped to popularize it, as did coverage in *Sports Illustrated* and ABC's *Wild World of Sports*.

No place in the world better epitomizes the agony of defeat than Pipeline. "It's a goddamn heartstopper," said **Rory Russell**, a top big-wave surfer from the '70s. **Gerry Lopez**, who surfed the tube with singular elegance and grace, admitted, "You're always hanging by your fingertips; you never really have it under control. But I guess that's the appeal of the place."

Joyce Hoffman, winner of five world titles between 1966 and 1971, succumbed to Pipeline's glamorous allure. With **Bud Browne**, noted surf photographer, filming from the shore, she saw it as her chance to be recognized as the first woman to surf Pipeline. But she got caught in it and lost her board and couldn't get out—"the rip was running like the Colorado River," she recalled. She had to be rescued by her surf mentor, **Phil Edwards**. It was an inglorious finale to her big-wave

debut—but at least she was caught on film in the tube, the deed recorded for posterity.

Pipeline has lost none of its sex appeal, its love for the camera. In the women's surfing film *Blue Crush*, the heroine goes out with her friend to surf Pipeline. Very sensibly, they select a place near a sand bar where the waves aren't quite as ferocious, and there is no coral to tear you to ribbons when you wipe out. One of the male surfers paddles over to her, hurling a challenge at her: "You want to surf Pipe? Pipe's over there!"

Of course, she rises to the challenge, and the viewing audience is treated to stunt double Rochelle Ballard tucking into the curl. It was just a movie, but the point was not lost on female surfers: no more hiding out by the sand bar, girls.

In 2005, ninety-six competitors, ranging in age from thirteen to forty-four, tested their mettle in the T&C Surf Women's Pipeline Championship. "Everybody said I was crazy putting on this event," said Betty Depolito, a.k.a. "Banzai Betty," who organized the contest. "For the past couple of years, I've been seriously watching Pipeline to see how the girls are doing and whether or not it was really feasible to hold an event here."

The winner in the longboard division was the oldest competitor—forty-four-year-old Kim Hamrock, a.k.a. Danger Woman. **The Californian, who has made it her personal business to push the sport higher and farther, followed her personal dictum to "take off and go fast," despite having broken her nose.** In the shortboard division, local Alana Blanchard came in first, fending off rival Rochelle Ballard. Said Depolito, "It's a hard spot to surf at any time. But they've really proven themselves."

Left: Katherine Carter surfing the North Shore. Right: Bringing out the "big gun."

JAWS

If Pipeline is the Hollywood bad boy of surf breaks, then Jaws is a young unknown director appreciated by aficionados for his dazzling special effects. Located on Maui's North Shore, Jaws refers to nothing mechanical; this is the real thing—crushing, grinding waves so fast and so immense that you have to be towed in on a Jet Ski in order to build sufficient speed to catch them.

When **Laird Hamilton**, one of the world's most celebrated big-wave riders, wiped out at Jaws, he said, "It vaporized me. I felt like my body went into little particles."

Kim Hamrock, a.k.a. Danger Woman.

Two surf instructors who work for Maui Surf Girls (MSG), which offers lessons and surf programs for women, became the first female tow-in team to ride the thirty-foot waves of Jaws. **Maria Souza,** an accomplished Brazilian water woman, had surfed Jaws with ex-husband Laird Hamilton ten years before. She and fellow Brazilian **Andrea Moller** trained for two years on the island's outer reefs in preparation to take on this fearsome break. Finally, in 2006, they felt themselves ready to take on this challenge. "I definitely note the pressure as a woman," Andrea Moller said, "but I'm just looking for the same thing the guys are—I want to feel the adrenaline rush out there."

Their accomplishment has pushed the limits of women's surfing, breaking yet another barrier—proving, if nothing else, that this madness called big-wave surfing is not gender-specific.

MAVERICK'S

It is the stuff of legend, a cold, dark, roiling force of nature that pounds the headlands just west of Half Moon Bay, California. As of 2006, it was the only surf break with its own Web site. A modern-dance interpretation was named for it. And it has at least one kill to its credit.

Linda Benson, a pioneer female surfer, is no slouch when it comes to big waves. She was, after all, the first woman to surf Waimea on Oahu's North Shore. However, when she speaks of Maverick's, it is in hushed, almost reverential tones: "Those waves are gnarly."

Maverick's lies dormant through the summer, flat and glassy, docile. Cats could surf here. Then, in late October, as the winter storms begin to build in the eastern Pacific, it starts to gather itself, feeding on the swells of energy, and by February, great thunderous sets of thirty- to

Sarah Gerhardt (right) heads down to Maverick's with husband, Mike Gerhardt (center) and John Raymond.

forty-foot waves beckon surfers from around the world. They show up with their wetsuits (the water temperature in winter hovers around fifty degrees, a stark formula for hypothermia) and paddle out into the teeth of this monster.

In 1994, **Mark Foo**, a celebrated big-wave rider from Hawaii, wiped out on a fifteen-footer and was dragged down into the cold, dark depths, where he breathed his last. "It just goes to show," said **Jeff Clark**, who pioneered surfing at Maverick's in the 1970s, "that no matter how prepared you are, you're in Neptune's playground."

Fifty miles south of Maverick's, in a quiet neighborhood in Santa Cruz, there is a trim yellow house with a pillowy sign on the door: Baby Sleeping. Another sign says, "Mahalo for removing your shoes." It is safe, quiet, protected from things that go bump in the night. Things like Maverick's.

"Mommy, tell me a bedtime story." Inside this snug cocoon, some dark night with the fog rolling in off the ocean, the baby will not sleep and he will beg for a story, and so she begins:

"Once upon a time, Mommy went to this place that has these giant waves . . . "

Sarah Gerhardt is not your typical female surfer. She is not blonde. She is not competitive (at least not in the conventional sense). She can talk surfing for over an hour without once uttering the words "stoked" or "gnarly." In fact, Sarah Gerhardt is not your typical anything. As a youth, she took care of a paraplegic mother. She has a PhD in chemistry. And she was the first woman to surf Maverick's.

She is sitting in her cozy living room with her husband, Mike, himself a big-wave surfer, and they laugh politely when asked if insanity runs in both their families. They admit that there are dangers in surfing Maverick's, but with preparation and experience, you take a calculated risk.

Sarah and Mike do not rush into things headlong. Before they decided to have kids, they got a cat, and that went well—though the cat has grown up with a very skeptical attitude about this surfing business. So they decided to have a child, and that went well, so now Sarah is carrying their second, and she has incredible big-wave surf dreams.

Growing up in Pismo Beach, on California's central coast, Gerhardt was asthmatic and, as is the case with many children with childhood illnesses, compensated by competing in sports, despite the physical challenges. She couldn't participate in anything involving dust or animal hair, so track was out, and softball, and equestrian events. But the ocean was one place where she could test her limits, and she liked the freedom of it. In the morning, she would get her mother up and help her dress, and then she would surf before school. Surfing required an intense focus, and out in the ocean you weren't thinking about your problems, just the waves.

She went to college to study chemistry, and then to graduate school for her doctorate, and she gave up competitive surfing. But still it called to her, this place where she had found both solace and exhilaration. **She found herself drawn to the big waves—"I pick challenges," said the surfing PhD mother of two. In the '90s she went to Oahu's North Shore, and Ken Bradshaw took her out at Sunset.** "The experience gave me a heightened sense of living," she said, likening it to a combination of Zen meditation and bingeing on adrenaline.

At first she encountered much resistance from the guys, but ultimately she earned her place in the lineup, and her own nickname—"Here comes the babe,"

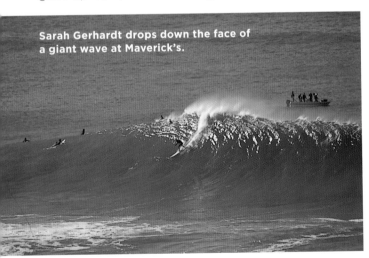

Sarah Gerhardt drops down the face of a giant wave at Maverick's.

they would say, in the way of males who don't quite know what to make of this girl in their midst (girl, midget, Gidget). In 1994, she saw Maverick's for the first time, and she was ready to give up everything, including grad school, to surf there. "I might get the daylights scared out of me," she recalls, "but I wanted to test my limits."

Sarah Gerhardt, surfing a big wave spot in northern Santa Cruz County, California.

Big-wave surf pioneer and scientist Dr. Sarah Gerhardt.

The first two times out, she didn't catch any waves. "It was very humbling," she says, "and I was not in the right head space." In between sets, she shared the ocean with whales and sea lions. About a mile out was a buoy, sounding its mournful tones ("ask not for whom the bell tolls"). **Then the set would come roaring in like a freight train. In 1999, she finally caught one. "This must be what it's like to do drugs," she says, hastily adding that she herself did not do drugs.**

"I don't live to surf," Gerhardt insists, a sentiment belied in her oft-quoted comment: "I'd surf in my toilet bowl if I could." Maverick's is no toilet bowl, and now that she has two kids, she will give it up, yes? No. She and Mike admit it—they need their fix. There are only about five days a year when conditions are optimal, and they monitor the surf reports, and when that day arrives when the waves are rolling in and the wind is from the north and the sky is clear, they bundle up the babies and off they go. While one watches the kids, the other surfs. Then they switch off. They are the only husband/wife surf duo at Maverick's.

Other big waves also beckon—Lower Trestles in San Clemente, Todos Santos in Baja, Pico Alto in Peru. Sunset is fun, but also the place where she had her worst wipeout. **It was hubris, she**

If they gave degrees in guts, Sarah Gerhardt would have two PhDs.

freely admits. "I could do no wrong," she recalled. "Then I made a rookie mistake." She looked up in time to see other surfers she was about to run over. She got slammed, losing a tooth and severing her lower lip. "It was hard to go back in," she admits. She did tow-in surfing with Ken Bradshaw at Gators, but now she finds that "paddle surfing is all the thrills I need."

Despite this almost holy devotion to surfing big waves, Sarah is leery of the tendency of surfers for it to be all about me. "I don't want to be that person," she says. She applauds the growth of surfing and the increase in sponsorship, but she misses the days when she was the only one in the water. "People burn me, cut me off," she says, the lament of many surfers today. **The unspoken question to these usurpers is, *Do you know who I am?* And the answer is no. Sarah Gerhardt is not a household name. Her wetsuit does not proclaim "First Woman to Surf Maverick's." Perhaps, if it did, they would make way.**

The next time she is out at Maverick's, and she hears the buoy, she asks not for whom the bell tolls: she has faith in herself, in her training and preparation, in her careful reading of conditions, her cumulative experience. Maverick's is, by now, interred in her bones, and it will be interred in the bones of her children, who slept in the womb as their mother dreamed of giant surf, who grew up on lullabies of big waves. ✳

Surfers brave the waves at Maverick's.

The Surf Breaks of the
APOCALYPSE:

Kim Hamrock comes by her nickname "Danger Woman" honestly.

CHAPTER 13

THE SEQUEL

THE ORIGINAL SURF BREAKS OF THE APOCALYPSE STILL COMMAND RESPECT AND AWE FROM BIG-WAVE SURFERS. PIPE IS STILL THE ULTIMATE PROVING GROUND. MAVERICK'S IS STILL THE COLD, DARK ABYSS TO WHICH BIG-WAVE SURFERS MAKE THEIR ANNUAL PILGRIMAGE. BUT THERE ARE OTHER BREAKS FAR-FLUNG ACROSS THE EARTH'S CIRCUMFERENCE, PLACES REMOTE AND FOREBODING WITH WAVES SO LARGE AND UNTAMED THAT YOU MUST BE TOWED IN. FEMALE BIG-WAVE RIDERS ARE FOLLOWING THE WAVES WITH THEIR BOARDS AND TOW-IN PARTNERS, WITH THEIR NERVE AND NEED FOR THE ULTIMATE ADRENALINE RUSH.

DUNGEONS

Dungeons, off of Hout Bay in Cape Town, South Africa, is a monster right-breaking wave that has been called the Southern Hemisphere's answer to Maverick's. Among the first women to tackle this forbidding break was **Kim Hamrock**—a.k.a. Danger Woman.

"Take off deep and go fast" is the philosophy of Hamrock, who came by her nickname honestly—back in the '70s, the surf was still a boys club—"Get out of here, bitch!" the guys would yell at her. But the Huntington Beach teen, small and fiercely determined, was not to be denied. You have to earn the waves, she realized, and so she gave back as good as she

Kim Hamrock.

got. The winner of six U.S. Surfing Championships in the 1990s and the 2002 Women's Longboard Champion, Hamrock gets in the face of anyone or anything—husband, guys on the surf line, sharks—that gets in her way. She pushes hard against her own limits and that of other women surfers. She has her own fierce brand of exhortation: "Pump it up, let's go!"

The same with big waves. In 1999, an invitation-only Longboard Tube Riding Competition, heretofore a men's-only competition, was held at Puerto Escondido. The male contestants were asked which woman to invite. Eight said Danger Woman, two said none. Hamrock's husband begged her not to go. She replied, "I want to!"

Her worst wipeout was Red Bull Big Wave Africa Contest, a forty-five-mile-per-hour wind whipping up waves of twenty to twenty-five feet. Hamrock got held down three times, but using a "flow, don't fight" strategy, she battled her way out of it.

Hamrock has a daughter, who in 2006 was seventeen. **"She is one of my heroes," Hamrock says, citing her favorite moment—when they rode the same wave together on a "Danger Woman" surfboard model. The maternal instinct is there, but equally powerful is her lust for big waves—she wants to surf the thirty- to forty-footers. "I hate loving it," she says. "I'm probably going to die, but what a way to go."**

XXL

Cut from the same cloth—small but filled with an almost furious reckless abandon—is Jamilah Star. At Waimea in November 2004, the Quiksilver Big Wave Invitational in Memory of Eddie Aikau was on hold, but there were surfers fool-hardy enough to go out. Most had to be rescued—but not "Jam." She made it out through the ten-foot shore pound without breaking her board, no mean feat on that wild, terrifying day. She surveyed the twenty- to thirty-foot swell and caught a monster wave and rode it in. "I was so excited I started dancing on my board at the end of the

Jamilah Star is a big-wave maven. Photographer Jim Russi.

wave—it was the most amazing day ever!" A California-born surfer who earned her chops on the surf break at Santa Cruz, Star celebrated like an NFL receiver who has just scored a touchdown, doing push-ups on the beach to the cheers of the crowd.

In 2006, the Billabong XXL Global Big Wave Awards for female surfers was a showdown between Jamilah Star and Hawaiian **Keala Kennelly**, who had surfed the tube at Teahupoo, Tahiti. Star, who also won in 2004, won the balloting by a

Jenny Useldinger, North Shore, Oahu, Hawai'i.

single vote and received the $5,000 winner's check for the second year in a row—hardly a lavish sum, but then, the big waves were never about the money.

Jennie Useldinger, like Jamilah Star, grew up in Santa Cruz, and she found that she shared Star's passion for the big waves. "It's a calling," she says. "I would feel guilty if I didn't."

She has surfed at Puerto Escondido on twenty- to thirty-foot waves. She has been towed in at Dungeons, with its huge cliffs and deep, cold water—and the sharks. In January 2005, she surfed Maverick's.

She has that big-wave surfer's attitude toward fear. "You enjoy the healthy fear—you harness it and use it in a healthy way."

Accidents do happen, however. In 2006, at Maverick's, she seemingly could do no wrong. *The ocean just loves me*, she thought. *I deserve this wave*. The ocean had its revenge; she tore her ACL. Her then-sponsor, Op, informed her that they would no longer require her services—"nothing personal" she was told. Roxy picked her up immediately and gave her the dream assignment—don't worry about competing, just surf, follow the waves. No limits were placed on her, no expectations. She was a wild card at the Roxy Pro at Sunset in 2006.

But it is not about competing, it's about being on the forefront of wave discovery. "Sometimes the harder route is better," she says. "I want to push my limits."

DO GIRLS HAVE THE CHOPS FOR CHOPES?

This question was posed by *Surfer* magazine in the wake of the ASP's cancellation of the 2007 Tahiti Pro. This contest was held at Teahupoo (Chopes), a break off the southern tip of Tahiti that surf journalist **Gary Taylor** described as "a freak of nature that some bastard decided to call a surf spot."

This Tahitian tempest has been known to reduce grown men to tears. Laird Hamilton took off on an eighteen-footer, the wave pouring over him like "liquid napalm"—he made it into the channel and sat and wept.

The men had been competing in the Tahiti Pro at Teahupoo since 1997; a women's division was added in 1999. In this, the ultimate test of youth versus seasoning and experience, of the fierce desire to win versus the equally

Keala Kennelly graces this big wave with her presence. Photographer Jim Russi.

compelling desire not to end up in a wheel chair writing their memoirs with a straw, it was the thirty-year-old Australian, **Melanie Redman-Carr**, who won over rival **Layne Beachley** and youthful compatriot **Chelsea Georgeson** by her willingness to risk a battering on the razor-sharp reef to eke out another fraction of a point.

Despite having proved themselves worthy adversaries of this surf break, the women have been consigned to the shore. In response to *Surfer* magazine's survey, Keala Kennelly, a renowned big-wave surfer, was scornful: "That is a ridiculous question. Teahupoo is dangerous for anyone who does not have the skills or drive to challenge themselves by attempting to ride it. What you are carting around between your legs is of no significance."

Sofia Mulanovich, while more circumspect in her response, expressed similar sentiments: "I think surfing Teahupoo is dangerous for anybody, but that doesn't mean people should stop surfing it. I was for sure really scared every time I was out there, but I think it was good for women's surfing to have that wave on tour 'cause it just pushed our surfing and made us more complete surfers."

Women will continue to surf Teahupoo, and Pipe and Waimea and Sunset and Jaws. They have proven that they are equal to the men in courage and daring. They know fear, but the fear is outmatched by the adrenaline rush. Despite the wipeouts and hold-downs, the bruises and broken limbs, they keep coming back for more—to get that adrenaline rush, to go out into the vastness of the ocean where there are waves that no one has ever surfed before. ✳

Rochelle Ballard loves a barrel.
Photographer Jim Russi.

BLACK / WHITE, MAN / WOMAN:
RACISM AND SEXISM IN WOMEN'S SURFING

IT'S AN EARLY FRIDAY MORNING IN JULY IN SOUTHERN CALIFORNIA. THE INTERIOR VALLEYS ARE BLAZING HOT, AS THOUGH SOMEONE PROPPED OPEN THE BACK DOOR TO HELL. BUT AT MALIBU, IT'S THIRTY DEGREES COOLER, AND THERE IS A SCRIM OF FOG HUGGING THE WATER. A LARGE CONTINGENT OF SURFERS IS OUT AT SURFRIDER. This is Gidget's beach. It looks much the same as it did fifty years ago: the crumbling wall, which in the day they called the Pit, a kind of surfers' holy wall, with boards propped against it. There is an air of serious purpose here: no kids with

CHAPTER 14

Andrea Kabwasa, Ventura, California.

shovels, no dogs frolicking in the water. If you want that, go around to the lagoon or up the coast to Zuma. This is a surfers' beach, and everyone knows it. **It is also a decidedly masculine place: a few ragged towels on the beach, guys getting into their wetsuits or rinsing off their boards. One little patch of sand suggests a feminine presence: there is an umbrella of faded white and yellow, and a towel neatly laid out, a backpack well stocked with water and healthy snacks.**

The surf is running in two- to four-foot sets at First Break, and through the fog, ghostly figures emerge, clad in black, cutting back and forth across the face of the waves, inscribing their mark. Around nine they start coming in (evidently, at that hour, surfers turn into corporate executives), but still no sign of the owner of the umbrella setup. Then, suddenly, a long, graceful figure rises up in the fog, trimming the wave with balletic ease, a stylish, elegant execution. After that ride, the surfer apparently is ready to call it a day and comes in. If it wasn't clear from the surfing style, it is now quite evident: it's a woman. Everything on her is black: the wetsuit, the hair, the skin.

A woman at Surfrider. A black woman. Tall, trim, in her thirties, Andrea Kabwasa took up surfing in San Diego in 2001. She had just returned to California from Toledo, Ohio, where she had been in an abusive relationship. She was starting her life over, rebuilding the self that had been damaged. On her thirty-second birthday, she had an epiphany: *I am not a victim. I can do whatever the hell I want.* So she took up surfing with an instructor who had been teaching people to surf for fifty years. Under his tutelage, and with her natural athletic ability (she played basketball at New Mexico State), she proved to be a quick study.

She migrated up the coast to L.A., and on her first day at Surfrider, she was nervous. She was there by herself, a black woman in a white guy's domain. How would she be received? She psyched herself up: **Don't let them intimidate you. You have every right to be here.**

Women of color are making waves of their own.

As soon as she set foot on the sacred sand, a man came running up to her. Was she going to be run off before she even set foot in the water?

"Sister, I'm **Rick Walker**, president of Black Surfers' Association."

Instead of being run off, she was immediately embraced and made to feel part of a surfing family, a group of African Americans, men and women, who surf the breaks along the Southern California coast. She paddled out and got in the lineup and caught her first wave, a kind of anointing: her new life had truly begun. As she gained confidence and expertise, she gained respect, and now she is considered one of the regulars.

This was so much better than at the gym. She got in a basketball game and became so frustrated with her poor performance that she kicked a wall and broke a toe. This was not good. She did not want to be that person anymore, impulsive, aggressive. Now she had another way to test her limits besides playing ball in a gym. Now she was a surfer, a soul-surfing sistah.

Australian surf instructor Jodie Barsby (right) and student (left) at the Roxy Jam.

"Surfing tamed my desire to always want to compete," she says.

Releasing her from this competitive impulse, surfing engendered in her a kind of spiritual awakening. There are no coincidences; there are paths that open up. At the same time, Andrea acknowledges, "The ocean reminds me that you can't be too cocky." It mirrors life itself: you take risks every day, you strive to overcome fears.

In surfing, she mostly found acceptance, but she did bear witness to the occasional racial slur; e.g., go back where you belong. Or more subtly: you really should go surf at a beginner's beach (this insult hits the trifecta: race, gender and competency). Once she saw a couple of white teenage boys attack an Asian woman surfer with their boards.

Andrea, who radiates empathy and calm, teaches special education at Los Angeles Unified School District and wants to bring her kids out to surf. In August she headed off to Scorpion Bay in Baja to surf and camp. In her spare time, she paints, and she is working on a line of T-shirts. She did a national print ad for Nissan and got paid $5,000 for her efforts: hardly a fortune but enough to pay her rent for the summer so that she could surf and paint. "Life is really not that serious," she says.

A young surfer checks out the waves.

As Andrea and others have ably demonstrated, blacks can and do surf. That fact would be lost on the likes of **Al Campanis**, former general manager of the Los Angeles Dodgers, who once famously remarked that the reason blacks don't swim is because they lack the buoyancy. This racial insensitivity, coupled with a lack of knowledge of the laws of physics (buoyancy is related to body fat, not skin color), cost Campanis his job. **The question of blacks and water, specifically surfing, was taken up in a more serious way on *Tavis Smiley*, the television talk show on PBS. The affable African American host and his guest, surfing mega-legend Laird Hamilton, tried to puzzle out why more African Americans don't surf. Smiley drew the obvious conclusion: it's about access and expense, and lack of surfing tradition. Blacks tend not to live at the beach. Surfboards cost money.** Hamilton, himself the epitome of the blond surfer, seemed bemused by this assessment: there are plenty of cheap boards, he insisted.

Hamilton missed the larger point, which is not so much about expense as a subtle cultural pro-scriptive that Campanis might have embraced: as the liturgy implies, surfing requires certain natural endowments; e.g., a bushy-bushy blond hairdo. Nor are there many African American surfing role models. In other sports previously the exclusive province of whites, blacks had proven themselves the equal—and in some cases—the superior of their white competitors—Tiger

Woods in golf, the Williams sisters in tennis. **But surfing remained curiously devoid of African Americans; there remained some hidden barrier that was yet to be penetrated.**

Race has figured into the women's pro surfing scene. In 1973, Hawaiian-born **Sharron Weber** canceled a trip to South Africa because her Hawaiian friends were barred from competing. (Evidently the irony of banning the very people whose ancestors were the first people to surf was lost on the South African organizers.) **Wendy Botha**, a South African surfer who was rookie of the year in 1985, faced the possibility of being barred from competing because of sanctions against South Africa due to the government's apartheid policies. In 1989, she changed her citizenship to Australia and captured her second world title.

With apartheid now officially ended, South African surfers such as **Rosy Hodge** can compete in events around the world. Rosy is tall and white and has long blonde hair—which no doubt was among the factors that influenced Roxy International to sponsor her for the World Qualifying Series.

Gender, not race, was the chief obstacle encountered by **Sharon Schaefer**, a small, hyper-fit African American actor and stuntwoman who makes her home in Playa del Rey, California. Schaefer, who taught herself to surf in order to round her stunt repertoire, quickly learned the reality of women in a surf lineup dominated by men: **"They don't want you in the water. You learn to scream." She could scream, and she called her share of waves. She had the chops, having been a competitive swimmer in high school. She recalls walking into the stadium, the only black among the competitors, and heads turning and people staring: Who is that?** That is a girl who seems to embrace the unusual, the unique. One Christmas her father presented the family with a unicycle, and Sharon would practice riding it for hours.

She became proficient enough in surfing to interrupt her stunt career to go out on tour. She had sponsors—*Vibe* magazine wrote her checks so that she could go on the World Qualifying Surfing Tour. "I couldn't believe someone was paying me to surf," she says. In her own words, she became a "surf bum," giving herself over completely to this lifestyle.

Surfing takes a big board and a bigger heart.

Schaefer grew restless at the segregation that she encountered on tour—not racial, but gender. **The women hung together, and the men hung together, and the two groups didn't mix much. She missed the company of men. One of her best memories is partying with Kelly Slater, the hyper-talented doyen of men's surfing.** "He's cute," she says over and over, mystified by the men who seemed to prefer the skinny supermodels with their blank expressions and rude attitudes to the beautifully conditioned women surfers.

Even in the small community of African American surfers, she has encountered sexism. At a BSA event in Malibu in 2006, the women waited all day while the men had their heats, the familiar experience of being "treated like crap." She did not intend to participate in the event in 2007.

Schaefer discovered a new calling: working with inner-city kids, exposing them to the joy of surfing, steering them away from gangs and drugs, building their self-esteem. "I'm someone who looks like them," she says. She does surf camps with groups such as Stoked and Surf's Up. It does not pay well, but as she has learned, things seem to work out when you do them for free rather than for the money. "My gift is the smiles on their faces," she says. "You're having more fun than we are!" one of the kids told her.

She hopes to prove to these kids (and perhaps to herself) that African Americans are capable of excelling in this white-dominated sport. As she says, "There's nothing we can't do if you show us how."

For her personally, surfing is a form of meditation, of prayer. It keeps you fit, it cleanses physically and spiritually. "All the lessons of life are in the water," says this accomplished surfer who has surfed Puerto Escondido in Mexico and the Back Door of Pipeline and Log Cabin on Oahu's North Shore. It's politics: men/women, black/white. It's nature: knowing the ocean. It's empowerment: giving and receiving. It's respect: self, others, the ocean.

Black or white, Australian or South African, all women face the pervasive sexism in the surfing world. In an early issue, *Surfer* magazine inveighed against the growing number of women out on the surf line: "There's nothing worse than an inexperienced girl ruining a good ride by dropping in on the shoulder right in front of a surfer coming off a hot section." If a male were to "drop in" uninvited, presumably it would be bad, but not as bad; the mere presence of females threatened the hegemony of the all-male club.

Damien Hardman, the ASP men's world champion in 1989 and 1991, paid what he no doubt considered a compliment to the female surfing world: "That's the best I've ever seen a chick surf."

In the ironically titled "Bikini Issue" of *Surfer* magazine, Matt Warshaw leveled the full invective of his pen against this pervasive sexist attitude: **"The fact that a world champion can nonchalantly describe a person as 'chick' in an interview without recrimination only hints at the length, breadth and depth of sexism in surfing. Surfing's gender morals, in a word, suck. Hardman is champ; ignorance is king."**

Lynne Boyer had to battle a different kind of ignorance. She had wild red hair, and her boards were airbrushed with her signature ribbon pattern. And how she could surf. She was world champion in 1978 and '79, using a radical, attacking style to upend the great **Margo Oberg** from her pedestal.

Even as she pursued surfing greatness, Boyer was struggling to come to terms with her sexual identity. To discover, in your thirties, that you are attracted to women added to her sense of isolation and inner turmoil. "Being gay is a double whammy," she confided in an interview in *Pacific Longboarder*. **"You have to hide who you are and get into major game playing."**

Keren Katz drops in as her husband looks on.

Buoyed by family support, Boyer battled her addiction to alcohol and cocaine. She also rekindled her passion for art and discovered the ultimate curative: love. She met an oceanographer from Hungary who became her partner. "The best days of surfing don't beat sharing the moonrise or a sunset with someone you love," said Boyer, now a successful artist.

Today, women like Lynne Boyer might discover their sexual identity much sooner and feel less reticent about coming out to the others on the tour. "We don't hold grudges against girls who like girls," says **Layne Beachley**, of the attitude of the women on tour. "Whatever they do on their own time, it's fine with us."

Today, surfing flatters itself that it is the ultimate meritocracy. It's not about the color of your skin, or whether you happen to have a uterus, or if you are attracted to the same sex: it's all about how you handle yourself in the surf lineup, your knowledge and heart and skill. But there is still an us-them dichotomy, and it exists across race and gender: men-women, black-white, hetero-lesbian, young-old. These divisions seem to pale in comparison to the common bond: the love of surfing, the joy of being in the ocean, close to nature. Barriers to blacks and women are gradually coming down, impediments are fewer and fewer, yet for those who remain set apart, there will always be, at some level, a battle for acceptance, a struggle for respect. ✳

GIRLS ONLY

CHAPTER 15

SURFING SCHOOL ADVENTURE #1: 1975

Practicing paddling on shore.

THE PARENTS OF SIXTEEN-YEAR-OLD NANCY GREEN HAD DECIDED TO DISPATCH THEIR TEENAGE DAUGHTER TO THE CAMP OF HER CHOICE FOR THE SUMMER. INSTEAD OF THE USUAL MOUNTAIN RETREAT WITH CANOEING AND HIKING, NANCY CHOSE A SURF CAMP IN SOLANA BEACH. THE CAMP, IT TURNED OUT, WAS HELD AT THE SAN DIEGO MILITARY SCHOOL, AND SHE WAS THE ONLY GIRL IN A GROUP OF FORTY BOYS. HER DORM ROOM HAD NO CURTAINS, AND IT ALSO HAD A PEEPHOLE, OF WHICH THE BOYS MADE FREQUENT USE. The first week, she sat on the beach and watched while the boys surfed, or she lay in the sand and practiced paddling and standing up. Finally, the second week, she made it into the water, and after a couple of failed attempts, managed to stand up; by the end of the day, she was surfing as well, if not better, than the boys. Gradually the novelty of having a girl among them wore off, and they started treating her with a modicum of respect.

Then another girl showed up, and they teamed up to punish their tormentors—water-soaked towels; fire extinguishers used as armaments to defend their room; bugs in the boys' beds. In retaliation, the boys made them watch *Jaws*, the Spielberg film about a predatory great white shark that had scared everyone out of the ocean. Filled with visceral terror, they were ordered to go night surfing. Under a full moon, in inky black water, they paddled out and discovered, to their horror, a sailor suit floating in the kelp. Terrified, they beat a hasty retreat to the shore. But they knew, the boys knew (and maybe even Spielberg's mechanical shark knew): girls could surf as well or better than the boys.

SURFING SCHOOL ADVENTURE #2: 2005

Inspired by a talk by **Kathy Kohner**, a.k.a. "Gidget," **Karen York** decided to attend Las Olas Surf Safaris for Women, located on a beach near Puerto Vallarta (the exact location remains a closely guarded secret). She and her fellow "surf sisters" discovered—or rediscovered—a sense of play, their surf instruction administered in a caring, nurturing environment; the rest of the time was occupied with delicious meals, yoga and even massages.

"With such care taken to create a physically and emotionally safe 'space,'" wrote York, "wonderful things begin to happen.

"Energy, rather than being used to deal with one's day-to-day responsibilities, is released to overcome self-consciousness and fear and to quiet those negative inner voices that keep us from taking risks or leaving our comfort zone.

"Not everyone stood up on the first day, or even on the second. Yet, one by one, with the expert coaching of our patient and persistent instructors, we rose to our feet. I must admit, it took me longer than most to 'get it' and 'get up.' Suffice it to say that after innumerable 'wipeouts' and inelegant knee stands, I eventually attained a vertical position, balancing precariously as I glided gloriously shoreward to the supportive cheers of my darling and daring surf sisters!"

Las Olas, the first in a growing number of surf schools and camps that cater to women, was cofounded by Bev Sanders. **While vacationing in Hawaii, the forty-four-year-old Sanders saw an ad with a picture of a dog riding a surfboard. The caption read: "If a dog can surf, so can you." Of course, the dog is on all fours, but it's a fine distinction.** Sanders took a lesson and discovered both a passion and an idea for a new business. She and her husband had a snowboarding business, which, not surprisingly, is very male dominated, with much "competition and posturing," whereas women's surfing has much more of a cooperative environment. "I never came across

Karen York tests her new skills on the waves.

Balancing act.

such camaraderie," Sanders said. She cofounded Las Olas with **Izzy Tihanyi**, of Surf Divas, a women's surf school whose cheerful floral logo is a familiar sight in La Jolla, California. **They happened upon a formula for success that has been emulated by other surf camps: offer women the opportunity to learn to surf, but also provide an environment in which they can bond, enjoy each other's company and otherwise partake of the good things in life.** No cold showers, no rooms with peepholes, no solitary meals in the cafeteria. The showers are hot, the food is first-rate and if there are aches and pains from the day's endeavors, there is a masseuse to massage them away.

Following the Sanders blueprint was **Chelsea Rostill-Huntley**, founder of the first all-female surf camp in Indonesia. She envisioned a place where women could unwind from the pressures of daily life and learn to surf in a supportive environment—what other name could she give it but Surf Goddess Retreats? "The thing we have in common is our deep connection and love of the ocean and riding its waves," says Rostill-Huntley. "Something wonderful happens when women surf: we grow more confident in ourselves, we find new places in our soul, we see the big picture of our lives and our place in it."

In addition to feeding the inner soul and fostering personal growth, Rostill-Huntley also recognized women's love of their creature comforts: no cold showers and beer, which the hard-core male surfer accepts as his dues at the end of the day. **Surf goddesses are put up in a five-star resort overlooking the Indian Ocean, offering private suites and villas with private plunge pools for those who don't want to put a crimp in the indulgence. They can revive their goddess physiques with Pilates and yoga and traditional Balinese massages. A portion of the profits goes to the saving of wild green sea turtles; whenever possible, guests join in the ritual of releasing the saved turtles back into the ocean.**

SURFING SCHOOL ADVENTURE #3: 2006

Patricia Beck did not surf until she was twenty. Growing up in California in the '70s, she was one of the girls on the shore who worked on her tan while the guys were out surfing. Then she went to Hawaii with her boyfriend, and she spent five days sitting on the sand while he surfed. "I was pissed," she states flatly. She came back to California and took up surfing and became an accomplished longboarder, competing in amateur events. **She remains a devotee of the longboard, preferring its graceful lines to the aggressive shortboard shredding. "It's an awesome, intimate connection to the ocean," she says.**

A former PE teacher as well as a mother of a two-year-old daughter, Patricia instructs women of all ages. But what about these two fifty-something women who have shown up on a sparkling morning on Labor Day weekend at Mondo's, just north of Ventura? Mondo's is known as an "Old Ladies" beach for its gentle break, ideally suited for beginners. One is Rebeca Avila, a mother of two from Arroyo Grande on California's Central Coast, and I am the other.

Neither of us had fully recovered from the humiliation we had suffered the year before at Turtle Bay on Oahu's North Shore. Rebeca was turning fifty and had always wanted to try surfing, so an excursion was mounted to the North Shore. On that Saturday in late October, only a few hours as a fifty-year-old, she went out for her first surfing lesson. The teacher was a young kid, less than enthused about trying to coax these two middle-aged women into standing up on a surfboard. It was a long paddle out to the first break, and the waves weren't terribly forgiving of a beginner's uncertainties. Rebeca was more concerned about her son David, eleven, who was also having a lesson. Her anxieties were quickly relieved; naturally athletic and a skateboarder, David popped up on his board and surfed like he'd been doing it all his life. After a two-hour struggle, Rebeca finally stood up for a second, dutifully cheered on by husband and sister on the bluffs. "This is the hardest thing I've ever done," said the mother of two.

Hats off to the surfing women of Las Olas.

Now, nearly a year later, we are attempting it again, this time with a woman teacher who, we're hoping, will have more patience with our shortcomings and perhaps help us to achieve that impossible dream: to ride the waves.

"If you catch one wave, it's a good day," Patty informs us, a philosophy of reasonable expectations. She has us don wetsuits, which she has provided for the lesson. How we have been dreading this part, but we struggle into our rubber outerwear and zip up, grateful that the beach does not come with a 360-degree mirror.

The tutorial on shore instructs in reading the waves, which are right-breaking, and observing safety rules and proper surf etiquette. "This is a beginner's beach," she reminds us, "and no one has control of their boards."

Including us. Our boards are nine-foot slabs of foam, broad and cushy as the front seat of a Buick. We practice our pop-ups; or rather, Patty demonstrates the pop-up, that fluid motion in which you push up on the board and then spring up into position. Rebeca and I are not of an age or physical condition where we can pop up with such ease. For us, it's more of a slow, evolutionary process, like that poster of the stages of man: first you are on

Bev Sanders, cofounder of Las Olas Surfing School.

all fours, then crouching like Cro-Magnon in his cave, then reluctantly ascending into a standing position. "Well," Patricia says, watching our agonizing progression, "practice your pop-ups at home."

The time has arrived. We drag our boards down to the water's edge and in we go. One forgets that in Southern California, with its benign sunny climate, the Pacific is fed by chilled Alaskan currents and even in late summer is in the mid-60s. In this instance, subcutaneous fat does not provide sufficient insulation; we are grateful for our wetsuits.

We walk out on the sandy bottom with our boards, dodging the incoming waves, and position ourselves in the ragged lineup. It becomes quickly apparent that, of the dozen or so surfers already out there, we are easily the worst. The two little boys receiving instructions from their father have the agility and fearlessness of youth. Our muscle memory reflects the caution and slowed reflexes of middle age. But hey, we're out there, cheered on by Patty. "Good job," she calls out when we approximate a skill such as paddling or pushing up off the board when a wave comes. "Good job!"—It's the same phrase I often hear mothers use with their young children to reinforce good behavior, but out here, we are but children, learning our ABCs and trying to stay out of the grown-ups' way.

After our first few attempts at catching a wave and standing up, Rebeca reports that "it's one thing to stand up, it's another to stay up." The physics of surfing is one of gravity; unless you can arrange your feet and place your body in perfect balance, you will fall off. Like Newton's apples, we fall, plopping into the surf with no particular grace. "Good use of your skills!" Patty calls out as I surface from one particularly graceless wipeout. She is referring to covering your head with your arms as you come up out of the water. It was, I assure her, pure instinct.

The first hour is spent in clumsy attempts to stand up, then falling down and paddling back out; but what better place to be than in the ocean on this glorious morning, the cold forgotten, the sun beaming down, birds wheeling overhead, seaweed brushing gently against our legs, the other surfers forgiving of our getting in the way. **It is true, of surfing, that whatever your troubles on the shore—work, kids, husbands, bills, the test results not back from the lab—all that is forgotten, and you are focused on this one thing, which is physically and mentally demanding but is also cleansing and productive of a sense of well-being.**

Patty teaches us a couple of new skills—the egg beater, in which you straddle the board and propel yourself around into position for the wave; and the turtle roll, in which, if you're outside and faced with a big oncoming wave, you roll over with your board so that it acts as a protective shell. Rebeca and I assure her that we will never confront waves big enough to require the turtle roll; we will confine ourselves to California rolls at a sushi bar. At least we make her laugh.

The last wave of the day. I am gripping the rails (sides) of my board, determined to have a good ride. I hear the rush of water behind me and start paddling furiously; I push up and almost have myself into a standing position when the wave collapses underneath me, like someone has shut off a valve. A closeout, it's called. "That happens," Patricia says. "The conditions today were kind of tough."

Others don't seem to be having a problem, but we take comfort from her words; and as we peel out of our wetsuits, we find ourselves happily in that surfer's cliché—we are stoked.

SB SURF GIRLS

The Santa Barbara Surf Girls have gathered at Mondo's for an afternoon surf lesson. The newly formed club has planted its flag, a pink banner that says "SB Surf Girls," and the four members who signed up for the lesson are struggling into their wetsuits. **Kristen Walker**, thirty, the founder and president, went to the University of Santa Barbara, then moved to Palm Springs. She has returned to the coast and taken up surfing. But she found that she did not care for surfing by herself, so she went online and found other women, also beginners, who wanted to have other women of similar skill level who didn't want to brave the surf lineup by themselves.

They are in their late twenties and early thirties, the SB Surf Girls. One is a lawyer, one is a Web developer, one lived in Antarctica and rappelled from helicopters. They are having fun with this notion of a club, naming their surfboards—Kristen's nine-foot foam board is called the Pink Lady. Lisa's is Purple Haze and Megan's is Cocktail.

On this sun-drenched afternoon at Mondo's, the waves are running two to three feet, and there are more than fifty surfers of varying skill levels out in the water, jockeying for waves.

They walk their boards out to the first break, with Patty, their instructor, standing in the water in her wetsuit to guide her pupils. Megan, a long-legged redhead, proves a natural and catches several waves, the others cheering her on from the shore. That had been her goal—to catch a wave on her own.

Lisa gamely tries to stand but ends up riding in on her knees. This is what the group refers to as a "Monica Lewinsky," a reference to the White House intern whose sexual liaison with Bill Clinton in the 1990s erupted into scandal. It's all in good fun, which seems to be the guiding spirit of this group of women.

"You learn so much about the ocean, and about life," Kristen says, standing on the beach in her bikini.

They stand there, watching the swells building from a tropical storm off Baja, the sun glinting off the waves, the perfection of a summer afternoon in Southern California. They look at each other, seized by a sudden epiphany: "We can surf 'til we die!" ✳

Inspiration: Zeuf

If you were to give a name to the goddess of surfing, perhaps it would be this name—Zeuf. One sees a proud Roman visage, a woman of extraordinary powers, on her surfboard, riding the waves. Indeed, the story of Zeuf, a.k.a. Robin Janiszeufski, is like a tale from surfing mythology in its unlikely coincidences, its dark portent of mortality.

But the heroine of this tale is a goddess of flesh and blood, living not on Olympus or some mythic place, but in Santa Cruz, California, and she wanted to be as amphibious as possible. She loved being in the ocean, and then came that day the thing that lurks beneath the surface—our darkest fear—caught at her and threatened to pull her under.

There is a lump on the surface of her breast. She wants to ignore it, but she is a CCU nurse and knows that would be folly. Breast cancer is the ultimate wipeout—to fight it, she will need to summon every ounce of strength that she possesses, and there had best be more where that came from.

The doctors came with their instruments and took the breast, and then there was chemo, this toxin that (Zeuf knows this) will in our lifetime become as archaic and unthinkable as feudal bloodletting. But for now, it is all they have, these terrible potions, these maiming instruments.

Zeuf subjects herself to this cruel regimen, but she knows from whence her strength comes, and it is not from a laboratory but from the mother source of life: the ocean.

She turned to the Heart of the Sea, to Auntie Rell, the guiding spirit of women's surfing. Rell Sunn, the legendary Hawaiian water woman, had breast cancer, and she had been put on the rack, but she had come back. On a visit to the Islands, Zeuf met her, and they surfed together and ate and laughed and told stories—and now Rell was her guide to cross the River Styx. Rell imparted her wisdom (an earned wisdom)—go to the ocean, in the water is where you will heal.

The doctors inserted a porta-catheter high in her chest so that, while undergoing chemo, she could continue to surf at her favorite break at Santa Cruz.

Zeuf gave herself over to the ocean and to the caring embrace of her fellow surfers. "Surfing provided everything I needed to heal," she said. "I loved being in the ocean; it was my savior."

Zeuf is an old soul, an optimist who adamantly refused to be viewed as a victim. "Cancer is not all of who I am," she insists. "It's just a chapter in my life." She was not about to wear it on her sleeve; indeed, she was determined to "let people see my strength and not my weakness."

Friend and filmmaker Charlotte Lagarde made an award-winning student film, *Zeuf*—a compressed four minutes of resolve and triumph. In one dramatic moment, Zeuf reaches inside her wetsuit and removes her prothesis. **A bold gesture of liberation, it signals acceptance of her body, embracing her identity as a woman.**

The cancer comes back. There is another debilitating regimen of chemo. Zeuf weathers this as well. Perhaps because of her intimacy with her own mortality, she is not afraid of dying. "There is a through line between life and death," she says. This acute awareness of life as a delicate fabric has led her to ponder the larger meaning of her own existence. "If I do die—what have I done? Have I provided a good example? I push myself really hard to be a good person."

She craves experiences, not things. "I view life as a process of experiencing rather than procuring," she says. From someone else this might sound priggish and self-righteous; Zeuf says it matter-of-factly, with a quiet assurance. As a CCU nurse, she is working to develop an integrated medical team in which alternative healing methods—acupuncture, meditation, yoga—are used to augment conventional Western treatments. Believing that there needs to be a spiritual approach to medicine, she asks the question, What broke your heart? How can you heal?

Every day is a gift: A smiling Zeuf (above, right) paddles out with Ashley Lloyd at Santa Cruz and catches a wave (below, left).

She heals by living life. She delights in the sensory experience of surfing, likening it to chocolate—"bright, fluffy, but big flavor." She surrounds herself with family and friends, in particular her ocean friends. She looks forward to the big waves every winter. She wants to surf with her husband in the Solomon Islands. She wants to go to Africa to do health care. In a word, her goal is as it has always been: to be as amphibious as possible. She does not aspire to Olympian heights, to surf-goddess status. She does not yearn for fame or fortune. She is not eagerly waiting for *Zeuf: The Musical* to open on Broadway. Nor is she sitting around waiting for the Grim Reaper. He will come as he does to all of us, in his time, but not today.

On a warm September afternoon, the sun has begun its autumnal descent to the horizon, a phlange of golden light spreading across the water. Zeuf has come down to Cardiff with her friends to attend the Roxy Jam, but now the tents have been struck, the people have gone home, and she has lingered behind to catch the last waves of the day. She paddles out, and Liz, and Ash, and they surf for the pure joy of it, being in the ocean with their fellow surfers, their boards battered but true, like old friends. **And they will spend the night in their vans or campers, and they will head north and surf San Onofre, and maybe Malibu: so many surf breaks, so little time, but they make time, for they know they are upon this earth but for a blink of an eye. Each day is a gift, every wave a blessing.** ✳

On the Shore No More

Women's surfing is a journey, both glorious and difficult. It has taken us to far-flung places around the globe and to secret places within ourselves. It has proven to a doubting world that we can hold our own in the surf lineup, that we are every bit as fearless and determined as the guys. It has brought us freedom, confidence, exhilaration. It is a passion, an addiction, a calling. Surfing is in our blood, interred in our bones, and so it shall be for our daughters and their daughters. If we are seen on the shore, it is because we are studying the ocean, taking our measure of the waves, resting before paddling back out. But we will paddle out, and we will have our portion.

Let us listen to the voices of women surfers, a heartfelt paean to the surfer within us all:

"If the guys were gonna go out, I was gonna go out." —Linda Benson

"Guys used to say, 'Chicks can't surf.' Well, we've proven that totally wrong. We're testing ourselves, expanding our abilities." —Layne Beachley

"Surfing is art on waves, a form of self-expression." —Lisa Andersen

"Surfing is a dream. It is freedom of movement, expression, time." —Jodi Young Wilmott

"Why would a woman surf? Why would a woman eat Belgian chocolate? Make love? Stay in bed all morning long? Because it's delicious, that's why." —Mary Osborne, *Sister Surfer*

"When the sets rolled in, it just didn't seem big enough." —Sarah Gerhardt

"I'm probably going to die, but what a way to go!" —Kim Hamrock

"The ocean is the great leveler. It doesn't matter who you are." —Zeuf

"Surfing is my time to be alone in the water and talk to God." —Daize Shayne

"If I could ride a wave in my toilet bowl, I would." —Sarah Gerhardt

"It's self-affirming to be in the water." —Charlotte Lagarde

"Give a girl the opportunity and the time, and it will generate and bloom into something beautiful and something great." —Layne Beachley

"We each have the potential to make a positive, lasting impression on our world, despite how uncertain it can be. And I know that these strengths are joyfully discovered by the little girl inside who just loves to play in the waves." —Bev Sanders, Founder, Las Olas

"You give waves instead of taking." —Jan, a Santa Barbara surfer

"The Gidget is inside." —Sally Field, *Accidental Icon*

"Enjoy the ride and love the ocean." —Linda Benson

In the generosity of spirit that is the embodiment of the female surfer, we will let a guy have the last word:

"After what I saw today, I only have this to say: Women rock!" —Skip Frye